LOST

BURLINGTON

VERMONT

LOST
BURLINGTON
VERMONT

BOB BLANCHARD

THE
History
PRESS

Published by The History Press
Charleston, SC
www.historypress.com

Front cover: Courtesy of Champlain College Special Collections.
Back cover: Courtesy of UVM Silver Special Collections; *insert*: University of
Vermont Silver Special Collections.

First published 2023

Manufactured in the United States

ISBN 9781467152297

Library of Congress Control Number: 2022949551

CONTENTS

CONTENTS

ACKNOWLEDGEMENTS

First, I want to thank Glenn Fay for recommending me to The History Press. Without him, this book never would have happened.

Next, thanks to the people who helped to put this book together, starting with Erica Donnis of Champlain College Special Collections, for her excellent work on the cover image. Special thanks to Prudence Doherty, Sharon Thayer and Chris Burns at UVM Silver Special Collections, for their patience and assistance during my many visits to the incredible trove of local history that they administer.

To James Blanchard, my "unofficial editor"—thanks for your time and suggestions to improve the manuscript. My appreciation also goes out to my official editor, Mike Kinsella, and all of the crew at The History Press.

Thanks also to Tom Little, Deb Joecks, Emily Speiser, the Vermont Historical Society, the archives of the Burlington Catholic Diocese, the Library of Congress, the archives of the Shelburne Museum and Joe McNeil, for providing images or information.

And finally, special thanks to my family, Linda, James, John, Viki and Luna. You guys keep me going.

For Luna.

INTRODUCTION

L ike many cities settled before 1800, Burlington, Vermont, has a great
    architectural legacy. The city has an abundance of nineteenth- and
    early twentieth-century mansions and grand homes, far more than one
would expect for a city its size. This is mainly due to the outsized prosperity
that Burlington enjoyed, from its early days to the present. Burlington's
prosperity largely flowed from its location on Lake Champlain. The city's
booming waterfront industries of its early years generated many fortunes,
and the wealthy elite of the town erected homes that were a way to display
their success. Burlington is lucky in that the vast majority of these great old
homes are preserved much as they appeared when first built. A few have
been lost, but by and large, these homes, in a wide variety of architectural
styles, appear much as they did in the time when they were constructed.

But over the years, Burlington has lost a great many nonresidential
structures that were important architecturally and historically, drastically
changing the look of the area around the city's downtown core. City
landmarks have been lost to neglect, demolished in the name of efficiency
or progress, torn down for parking lots or lost to the main culprit: fire. This
volume will re-create for the reader in words and pictures the history of
many of these lost structures, from the time they were built until their loss.

1

THE CITY OF BURLINGTON

Burlington, Vermont, known as the "Queen City," occupies one of the most beautiful sites of any city in the United States. It sits on the eastern shore of Lake Champlain, the largest freshwater lake in the country after the Great Lakes. This 121-mile-long ribbon of water is oriented north to south and very narrow along much of its span. Burlington sits at the lake's widest point, a 12-mile-wide expanse of water known to locals as the "broad lake."

Beyond Champlain's waters to the west are the high peaks of the Adirondack Mountains. This combination of water and mountain makes for an unforgettable vista from the city that generations of travelers have marveled at.

Author Henry James weighed in from an 1870 visit: "The vast reach of the lake and the double mountain view go far to make Burlington a supremely beautiful town." Other noted authors, from Nathaniel Hawthorne to William Dean Howells, have remarked on the beauty of the city's location.

As a writer for *Frank Leslie's Illustrated Newspaper* put it in 1883: "Among our smaller inland cities few are so highly favored as Burlington, Vermont. Its situation on an amphitheater sloping up from Lake Champlain, and girt with mountains on all sides, is surpassingly beautiful. Favorably placed for commercial and manufacturing enterprises, and having been the seat of a university since the beginning of the century, it has a population whose wealth and taste are indicated by elegant residences and grounds, and a high degree of social refinement."

The city rises steeply from the water's edge to a point about three hundred feet above the lake at the top of what is known as "The Hill." From there, the city flattens out to the east, and the view of the Green Mountains comes into sight. Burlington has beautiful panoramas both to its east and to the west.

But in the late 1700s, Burlington was nearly unreachable. The area was total wilderness; a journey to it was the stuff of pioneers. One of the city's first settlers, Horace Loomis, recorded his family's journey to Burlington from Massachusetts in 1790. They traveled nearly the entire length of the frozen Lake Champlain. Even an arduous winter journey like that was easier than getting to Burlington over land, which was covered by unbroken old-growth forest. In Burlington, Loomis found a village with a few log huts along the lakeshore, one of which was a tavern.

The early inhabitants of Vermont came chiefly from southern New England, and they tended to settle in southern Vermont, a much shorter trip and a climate similar to what they were used to. It's doubtful that many even knew there was such a place as Burlington in Vermont, and it's even more doubtful that they would have endured the additional travails required to get to that much more remote village.

But it is the lake and that western view that have shaped the city over its entire existence. The lake had served as a highway for Native tribes long before European settlement of the area. Then the French and, later, the British used the lake for wartime incursions from Canada, causing the area to play an important role in the early history of America.

After the threat from British troops in Canada subsided following the War of 1812, the role of the lake in commerce started to become much more significant. Early trade consisted largely of rafts of lumber being floated to Canada (Lake Champlain flows north) via the Richelieu River. But the opening of the Champlain Canal in 1823, linking southern Lake Champlain with the Hudson River, quickly changed that, as most Burlington commerce started flowing to and from major American markets like Albany and New York City.

The first census to include Vermont, in 1790, showed a total of 332 people in Burlington. Ten years later, the population was only 815, putting Burlington in eighty-third place among Vermont towns. But the opening of the canal changed everything. The city started to grow more rapidly, and by 1832, it was the most populous town in the state, a position it would not relinquish.

All sorts of goods started coming to Burlington via the canal, while the major commodity shipped south from the city was lumber. Logs from the inexhaustible forests of Canada came to Burlington, where they were processed into lumber and other articles for shipment to the southern markets to supply the needs of a rapidly growing country.

This trade in lumber would grow to the point that Burlington became the third-largest lumber port in the United States by volume, after only Chicago and Albany. Lumber and transport would create a business elite in Burlington whose wealth enabled them to build large mansions and estates, chiefly on the streets of what is known as The Hill section. Because the city slopes up from the lake, streets up on The Hill enjoyed beautiful views of the lake and mountains. The higher up the slope, the better the view, so some of the largest estates were at the very top of that hill, where the vistas were the finest. Street names like Prospect, Cliff, Summit and Bay View hark back to the days when just about any building lot on The Hill had a wonderful view. Over time that would change, as trees grew tall and so did buildings. But for a period roughly corresponding to what is called the Gilded Age in America, Burlington's elite built many beautiful and even spectacular homes on The Hill.

As Burlington's lumber industry matured, it branched out until all sorts of building materials—moldings and mantels, doors and windows and all manner of ornamental trim—were produced in the city's waterfront mills. An abundance of skilled carpenters and stonemasons were also readily available. All of this resulted in the creation of an architectural legacy that is a continuing reminder of a bygone era. Homes of all types—Federal, Greek Revival, Victorian, Queen Anne, Shingle, French Second Empire and others—adorn the streets of Burlington's Hill section and other areas as well. Hundreds of homes with turrets, belvederes, ornate woodwork and porches and other hallmarks of bygone craftsmanship dot the streets of Burlington. The large number of architecturally significant buildings is remarkable for a city its size.

Burlington is fortunate that nearly all of its historic homes have survived. A few significant residences have been lost to fire, but the historic residential sections of the city are largely intact. The presence of the University of Vermont and Champlain College on Burlington's Hill has contributed greatly to the preservation of many old homes. These two institutions have acquired many historic homes and maintain them in a manner that would be nearly impossible for most individual owners.

But while most of the historic housing stock is intact, there have been significant losses. A great many of Burlington's historic public and commercial buildings from the nineteenth and early twentieth centuries have been lost, mostly in and around the central business district. The lost buildings range from cathedrals to schools and from charitable institutions to hotels, theaters and others. These lost structures were irreplaceable, the products of an era when public buildings were highly ornamental, with stone and wood carvings and other features that were common in their day but can't be duplicated now because of cost and the loss of the craftsmen capable of doing such work. This loss has greatly altered the look of the downtown area of Burlington. Since these buildings now exist only in photographs and memories, this volume will attempt to capture a bit of what it must have been like to live in a time when so many of these great buildings graced the city's streets.

It is not just lost buildings that are covered in this book. Lost streetscapes, changes in parks and a lost neighborhood are also discussed. One of the most drastic changes involved the Burlington waterfront itself. For over a century, it was an industrial waterfront, covered with mills and factories with belching chimneys, churning out products for the local and distant markets. Numerous passenger and freight trains chugged through the waterfront daily, along with canal boats and barges that continually came to and departed from the city's wharves with their cargoes. Later, oil tanks proliferated as the automotive age took hold. The waterfront was a bustling place that generated great wealth, but it was not an inviting place to take in the view. After the lumber and related industries died out, the previously bustling area became a derelict waterfront. In recent decades, the last vestiges of that former time have been removed, and an expansive, inviting public waterfront park has taken its place. But the industrial waterfront that generated the wealth that resulted in the building of Burlington's historic neighborhoods is where we will begin this examination of "Lost Burlington."

2

THE INDUSTRIAL WATERFRONT

Two events marked the beginning of Burlington's rise as a commercial port. First was the 1823 opening of the Champlain Canal linking Burlington to population centers to the south via the Hudson River. The second was the construction of a breakwater to protect Burlington's harbor from the prevailing westerly wind and waves. This massive project was begun in 1835 by the U.S. Army Corps of Engineers. Since the breakwater wasn't completed until 1890, it's safe to say that the opening of the Champlain Canal was the more important of the two events. This created access to southern markets and ignited the development of Burlington as an important lumber-processing center. Eventually, the Chambly Canal to the north of the lake provided access to tidewater to the north and the south.

The trade in lumber and wood products chiefly involved logs and lumber coming down from Canada, stopping off at Burlington for processing and then being shipped south via the Champlain Canal to retail markets. The chief activity was planing and otherwise "dressing" lumber. This activity could have easily been done in Canada by the Canadian lumber firms shipping the lumber south, all of which had significant mill complexes north of the border. This would have avoided the extra handling involved in the stop-off at Burlington, but Burlington benefited from a tariff passed in 1870 that placed a high tariff on dressed Canadian lumber. The tariff was shepherded through Congress by Vermont senator Justin Morrill and resulted in the construction of several large finishing mills along the Burlington waterfront and an explosion in the volume of rough lumber

The Burlington waterfront in the late 1800s. Trains, mills, factories and freight sheds cover the area. Canalboats are tied up at the wharf, and a passenger steamboat is docked at the pier next to the Lake Champlain Yacht Club clubhouse. The 1860s railroad depot is at the left. *Courtesy UVM Silver Special Collections.*

coming down from Canada. This in turn spurred a lot of ancillary activity as lumber-related manufacturers built facilities to produce furniture, moldings, doors, windows, trim and other products.

The processing of all of this lumber created mountains of wood shavings. One of the largest firms, Shepard and Morse, processed seventy-two million board feet of lumber annually and was said to generate thirty tons of shavings and sawdust daily. All of the city's lumber mills burned the shavings they generated to power their boilers. They had plenty left over to sell to non-lumber mills and factories, which likewise powered their boilers with this fuel, which was much cheaper than coal. Despite all of this, there were still plenty of shavings left over that needed to be disposed of. Mounds of shavings were a common sight on the waterfront, and teamsters were kept busy carting wagons full of shavings to various points in the city to be dumped. One of the main sites for dumping was Burlington's extensive ravine.

The industrial waterfront of the last half of the nineteenth century was a rough place. Again quoting from Henry James's 1870 visit: "The lower portion by the lake-side is savagely raw and shabby."

On the transport side, all of this activity called for the construction of wharves, freight sheds and terminals for the many cargo boats, passenger steamboats and, later, trains and barges coming into and going from Burlington.

All of this activity required space. One of the problems with Burlington's location was that the land sloped up steeply from the lake, with very little flat area suitable for building the many structures needed for the growth of the city's industrial waterfront. Over time, many dozens of acres of flat waterfront land were created using various methods. The railroads alone created twenty-three acres for their depot, tracks and freight sheds. Many more acres were added later, chiefly by oil companies for the oil tanks that would inhabit the waterfront when oil chiefly arrived at Burlington by barge.

At the peak of the lumber boom, this land was covered by factories and mills, but most of all, it was covered with stacks and stacks of lumber. Photos from that period show lumber stacked in every available part of the waterfront, even out onto piers. Huge stockpiles were required to get the mills through the winter, when the lake froze and canal boat traffic ended. There was so much lumber stacked on the waterfront that companies took to giving street numbers to the lanes between their stacks to enable employees to better keep track of where they were when they were out among the piles.

As the twentieth century went on, railroads replaced canal boats as the main means of transport for goods to and from Burlington. The end of the tariff on dressed lumber from Canada caused a dramatic change, as Canadian mills started doing their own planing, tongue and groove cutting and other tasks. The high tariff was the only reason that most of Burlington's dressing mills existed, and once that reason was eliminated, shipments of lumber from these mills no longer had any need to stop and unload at Burlington for processing.

Finally, the 1929 opening of the Champlain Bridge between Chimney Point in Vermont and Crown Point, New York, had an immediate effect on the steamboat business on Lake Champlain. Until this point, steamers had been the only way to get across the lake, so the lake steamboat business, which dated to 1809, had been prosperous for a very long time. The opening of the Champlain Bridge marked the beginning of the end for steamboats on the lake.

These events combined to render dramatic changes to the Burlington waterfront. Unused wharves fell into disrepair and became overgrown with vegetation. Lumber mills quickly closed and were left vacant, subject to neglect and deterioration. Oil tanks began to dominate the look of the

This 1860s view of the Burlington waterfront shows mill buildings and stacks of lumber covering the entire area. In the foreground, three men stand on an enormous pile of wood shavings. The Episcopal Institute can be seen in the distance rising above the lake. *Author's collection.*

waterfront to the north and south of Burlington Bay as petroleum products brought up by barges via the Champlain Canal were used to store large quantities of gasoline and heating oil. The acreage once covered by stacks of lumber became empty, weed-infested vacant lots. The area of Burlington around the breakwater, so long a bustling source of wealth, became derelict, occupied by empty factories, rotting piers and the sunken hulks of old vessels. The Lake Champlain Yacht Club, which had its clubhouse on the Burlington waterfront since 1888, fled Burlington for Shelburne Bay in 1936.

Burlington mayor John J. Burns made the cleanup of the waterfront a priority, as it had become an embarrassment to the city. In the early 1940s, his goals were mainly met, as the worst of the waterfront was mitigated. The steels hulks of sunken boats were raised as part of a World War II salvage drive, and the third and final Lake Champlain Yacht Club building, which had deteriorated badly, was disassembled by salvage crews.

But the waterfront was still far from attractive. It had become an empty wasteland, with dozens of large oil tanks, a scrap-metal yard and a railroad yard as the dominant features. It would take a long court battle to decide who owned all of those waterfront acres that had been created during the boom times but now sat empty. When that was finally settled in favor of the city, steps began to be taken to clean up the waterfront. This decades-long process involved the elimination of all of the oil tanks near the city proper, the closing of a coal-fired electric power plant, the installation of a floating public boathouse at the site of the long-ago Lake Champlain Yacht Club pier, a new Coast Guard station and, most important, the creation of acres of public parkland directly on the lake. Waterfront Park has become a jewel of Burlington, where for nearly a century and a half industry and then decline prevailed.

3

MANSIONS AND ESTATES

The majority of Burlington's most magnificent homes were built by wealthy local businessmen. The lumber industry and related manufacturing were the main sources of wealth, but fortunes were also made in banking, transport and other areas associated with an economic boom. Burlington's boom times were long-lasting—and so the number of great homes built was substantial—often spanning more than one generation. But the city also attracted several wealthy individuals who had made their fortunes elsewhere. They were attracted by the natural beauty of the city, and they built some of the largest estates in Burlington, often as summer residences. Several of those great estates remain, such as that of A.A. Buell (now UVM's Redstone Campus) and Henry Holt's Fairholt. But others have been lost.

OVERLAKE

We'll start with the largest lost estate that once stood in Burlington. This was Overlake, a fifty-six-acre estate that stood on the southern end of South Prospect Street. It was built by Colonel Legrand B. Cannon as a summer home (he wintered in New York City). Cannon was born in New York City but was raised and educated in Troy, New York. He had a successful career in railroads and with the Delaware and Hudson Canal Company.

Mansion house at the Overlake estate of Colonel Legrand B. Cannon. This is the west side of the mansion as seen in 1893. *Author's collection.*

An 1896 listing of the members of the Union League Club of New York City showed him to be one of the richest men in America. His net worth was shown as $6.5 million, easily making him a billionaire in today's money. He had been involved with the Lake Champlain Transportation Company as a director since 1856, a position that occasionally brought him to Burlington. That year, he was in town and was strolling with his brother-in-law on Prospect Street (then called Tuttle Street) when he came upon the panoramic view at the top of Cliff Street. He was so impressed that he purchased the property and had a large mansion constructed in 1858.

A contemporary account described the mansion as being built in the French Chateau style. It was designed by architect W.R. Bergholtz, who also laid out the extensive grounds. At this time, most of the city was treeless, making for unobstructed views of the panorama below, which stretched for one hundred miles, from Whiteface Mountain in New York to Montreal to the north.

The grounds featured gardens, rock ledges, a mile-long carriage road, walking trails, over three hundred trees that Cannon had planted and numerous outbuildings of varying sizes. The house stood above it all, a buff-colored, brick-and-stone monument to Cannon's wealth and also to his love for the area. He would return here every year for the rest of his long life, dying at Overlake two days after his ninety-first birthday, in 1906.

Cannon had four children, a son and three daughters. His son, Henry, predeceased him; otherwise, the fate of Overlake may have been different. None of his daughters were interested in living at or maintaining Overlake. They all were married and had their own homes. Only one, Marie, lived in Burlington, and she and her husband, Louis Clark, lived in a forty-five-room wood-frame mansion on a large southern section of the original Overlake estate that Colonel Cannon had given them as a wedding present. After the original Overlake mansion was no more, the Clark home also came to be known as Overlake.

There were attempts to sell the estate. Grenville Clark, Colonel Cannon's grandson and a prominent New York City attorney, listed it several times for sale or lease in publications specializing in large country homes. But Overlake found no takers. You would have had to come in person to see the view to be as taken by it as Colonel Cannon had been. You couldn't do it justice in a real estate ad.

So Colonel Cannon's beloved Overlake was unoccupied for most of the years between his death and its loss. It briefly served as a women's dormitory for the University of Vermont, but otherwise it sat neglected and decaying.

In 1923, a man named James H. Flinn came to Burlington. He was born at Overlake in 1873, probably the son of a servant. He had risen to a high position with the Famous Players-Lasky movie studio (the precursor to Paramount Pictures) and was scouting Overlake as a possible location for a movie shoot. He was so distressed at the condition of his birthplace that he composed a poem, "Overlake," dedicated to the late Colonel Cannon. It was written as an elegy, mourning the loss of what once was. In the absence of any press reports or photos of Overlake near the end of its time, the poem gives a sense of the state of the formerly majestic residence. Here are the first few verses as printed in the *Burlington Free Press*:

"Overlake"
(To L.G.B.C.)

On a terraced hillside looming
Like a beacon 'gainst the sky
Stands a stately mansion relic
Of a broken dynasty; melancholy
Is the silence that pervades its vacant
Halls, and the hand of time rests
Heavy on its fast decaying walls.
Like an aged sentry guarding jealously
Its acres vast, there are only empty
Echoes of a proud and honored past.

Barred its doors, its windows shuttered
Locked its crumbling entrance gate
Solitude and desolation linger round the
Old estate
Sad memento of a power sleeping
Never to awake, and the grandeur
Fled forever that belonged to Overlake.

He goes on to contrast the never-ending glories of the vistas spread out below with the relatively brief life of the once great house. Overlake did not end up being used as a movie location.

The end came in 1925, when it was announced that the estate would be subdivided into housing lots and the mansion torn down. The reporting of this announcement was very matter-of-fact, with no comment being made of the loss of this great historic residence. Decades would have to pass before the historic preservation movement made people recognize the need to preserve a place like Overlake. The first housing development that was built on the old estate's northern end is known as Overlake Park. Today, it is one of the most desirable neighborhoods in Burlington.

Along with the main building, all of the outbuildings were demolished, with two important exceptions. The estate's carriage barn and a caretaker's cottage, which sat next to each other at the far northeast corner of the property, were spared. Why these two were left standing is a mystery. Both have been converted into private homes. The four-thousand-square-foot carriage house

The carriage house / coachman's cottage is one of only two buildings that remain from the sprawling Overlake estate of LeGrand B. Cannon. *Vermont Historical Society.*

is made of brick and stone and mirrors the style of the Overlake mansion. That home was recently listed for $2,350,000, a testament to the quality of even the outbuildings on Colonel Cannon's estate.

The forty-five-room mansion on the southern end of the estate that Colonel Cannon had given to daughter Marie and Louis Clark as a wedding present is also gone. The 1884 building remained in the Clark family until 1962, when it was sold to the Overlake Day School, which had been running a school in the building since 1958. Eventually, that private school went out of business, and the vacant building burned in 1976. Fire officials said the blaze was almost certainly arson. A development called Overlake Condominiums was built on that portion of the estate.

FERN HILL

Fern Hill is the name given by John N. Pomeroy to the large home he constructed in Burlington in 1851. Pomeroy was born in 1792 in a log cabin in Burlington, the son of Dr. John Pomeroy, one of the earliest settlers in the city. John N. Pomeroy entered the University of Vermont when he was thirteen years old. Following graduation, he became a lawyer and practiced law for many years in Burlington. In 1844, his father died and left him a considerable fortune. As an early settler, Dr. Pomeroy had acquired a lot of land and became quite wealthy as the city grew and the value of his property increased.

With his newfound wealth, John N. Pomeroy resolved to build the home of his dreams. His selected location was on the same street as Overlake, the current Prospect Street. No doubt he picked the location for the same reason as Colonel Cannon did: the magnificent view from the top of Burlington's Hill section. But Pomeroy selected a lot at the far northern end of the street, far from Overlake at the southern end. Because the land sloped away from his building site not only to the west, but also to the north and the east, Pomeroy's home would have panoramic views not only of the Champlain Valley and Adirondack Mountains but also of Burlington's Intervale Winooski River floodplain, the city of Winooski and the Green Mountains to the east. The home was built on the east side of the street. Pomeroy also acquired the land across the street and kept it vacant, ensuring an unobstructed view of the lake and mountains. This was a common practice for large estates built on the street in the early days.

Construction began in 1848, and it took two years to complete. The home was a basic Italianate design with Greek Revival influences. The original house had twenty-two rooms. Like most of the great homes of Burlington, it featured a belvedere on top to provide an even higher vantage point from which to view the panoramas spread out below the home. The house featured beautiful formal gardens. Pomeroy spent the rest of his long life enjoying Fern Hill. He died in 1881 at the age of eighty-eight.

After Pomeroy's death, Fern Hill went through several owners, two of whom made additions to the original house. But as the twentieth century progressed, the number of people who wanted to live in a house the size of Fern Hill was rapidly diminishing. So in 1950, the Fern Hill estate was sold to the Ohavi Zedek synagogue of Burlington. They were mainly interested in the estate's considerable acreage, wanting to build a new synagogue for their congregation. So the following year, Ohavi Zedek sold the now

John N. Pomeroy's mansion, Fern Hill, at the end of North Prospect Street. When it was completed in 1850, it had sweeping views to the west, north and east. *Author's collection.*

twenty-five-room Fern Hill mansion to Phi Sigma Delta, a fraternity at the University of Vermont.

By the late 1960s, Phi Sigma Delta had closed its chapter at UVM and Fern Hill became vacant. For the next few years, it was plagued by constant trouble from squatters, vandals, illicit parties and the like. Ohavi Zedek reacquired the mansion in 1971 and attempted to protect Fern Hill by boarding it up to try to keep people out, but trouble persisted.

Finally, on the morning of Saturday, April 8, 1972, the front page of the *Burlington Free Press* read, "Fire Destroys Another Landmark." Fern Hill had been severely damaged in a fire the day before, a blaze that was almost certainly intentionally set. The headline references a recent spate of suspicious fires in Burlington that had consumed a number of historic structures. Unfortunately, John N. Pomeroy's beloved Fern Hill was added to that sad list, as it was bulldozed soon after the blaze.

THE FRANK R. WELLS ESTATE

The Frank R. Wells estate is unusual in many respects. It was the last great mansion built in Burlington. Also, unlike Fairholt, Overlake and Fern Hill, Wells's estate was never given a name, making it necessary to have to keep referring to it here as the "Frank R. Wells estate." Another unusual aspect of Wells's estate was its extremely short life. It lasted just a little over forty years.

Frank R. Wells was born into wealth. His father was prominent Civil War general William Wells, whose statue stands in Burlington's Battery Park and at Gettysburg. His uncle Edward Wells, William's brother, was one of the founding partners of Wells Richardson a patent medicine firm in Burlington. In later years, two other Wells brothers, Frederick and Henry, also joined the firm. Later, William served as president of the company.

The patent medicine business boomed in America for decades in the nineteenth century. Largely based on grossly exaggerated claims as to their effectiveness and the presence of alcohol in many concoctions, patent medicines were immensely popular until the Pure Food and Drug Act of 1906 brought about their decline.

But that act of Congress was far in the future when Wells Richardson was founded shortly after the Civil War. Its main product, Paine's Celery Compound, was able to rise above the crowd of other patent medicines as a result of the firm's relentless marketing. Its old printing facility, which still stands on lower Main Street, housed sixty-six printing presses that generated mountains of advertising material for the firm's products. In addition to its Burlington headquarters, Wells Richardson eventually had branches in Montreal, London and Sydney, Australia. No financial reports were ever required of this private firm, but it's safe to say that all of the partners became fabulously wealthy. They all built large mansions in Burlington's Hill section. Edward Wells's stone and brick mansion, now the University of Vermont's Alumni House, is probably the most magnificent private home ever built in the city. In addition, yachts and private islands added to the trappings of members of the Wells family.

Into this world came Frank R. Wells, the only son of William Wells. None of the other three Wells brothers in the Wells Richardson firm had a son who lived to adulthood, so Frank was the only Wells offspring of the second generation to enter the family business. When he became secretary of Wells Richardson in 1896, times were still good. He married California socialite Jean Mary Hush in 1900, and their honeymoon consisted of a six-month trip around the world, followed by weeks spent in New York for the opening of the show season.

On their return, they settled into life in Burlington. In 1907, Mrs. Wells gave birth to the couple's only child, a son named William, but he died after only three days of life. Frank stayed busy with work and civic activities while his wife kept a very low profile.

As he neared fifty, Frank decided to build a home on a grand scale on an equally impressive plot of land. This was despite the fact that the era of mansions and extensive grounds and servants was passing into history. He enlisted the New York architecture firm Mann and MacNeille to design it for him. From their design, a large brick and granite Georgian mansion was built in 1915. It featured a morning room and a sun porch on the south side and an extensive wing for servants on the east. The house stood on a fifteen-acre parcel of land a bit below the top of the Hill but still plenty high enough to have dazzling views. The estate was between Summit Street at its top and South Willard Street at the bottom. To the south was Cliff Street. The house was centered in the middle of the property, far from the sidewalks and roads.

The Georgian mansion of Frank R. Wells. Hidden from view for much of its existence, this grand home stood for only about forty years. Forty-four large homes now occupy this site, formerly the home of two people and their servants. *Author's collection.*

The west gate of the Frank R. Wells estate is overgrown with weeds. High above, the huge Wells mansion can be seen a short time before it was demolished. *Deb Joecks.*

The land sloped steeply down to the west of the house, ensuring that nothing would ever block the view. The grounds were manicured with low walls and gardens and eventually a swimming pool. There were several large areas of mature trees around the house.

As a result of all of this, the house could barely be seen from the street, and it became more hidden as the plantings and trees around it grew. As the years passed, most residents of the city didn't even know this mansion in the heart of the city existed. The couple became more reclusive as Mrs. Wells endured ill health in her later years. She died in 1941, and Frank passed away in 1956.

The couple had no surviving relatives, so their will left the entire estate to the nearby University of Vermont. But there were conditions attached to the bequest that probably doomed the mansion. The will stated that the mansion had to be used as either the home of the university president or a museum. In either case, it would be named the Jean Mary Hush Wells and Frank R. Wells Memorial. It was further stipulated that the mansion not be altered in any way.

UVM trustees declined the bequest, saying that the conditions imposed by the will were impractical. This set off a series of other proposals for the property. The Masons considered buying it. A hotel was proposed for the property. But finally, in late 1957, the estate was purchased by a doctor with connections to Burlington who also was engaged in real estate. He stated that he bought it because it was the largest piece of residential property remaining in the center of Burlington.

So the mansion was torn down only forty-two years after it was completed. Frank's attempt to preserve it as he built it had the unintended consequence of bringing about its destruction.

Prior to the demolition, the contents of the mansion were put up for sale. Area residents flocked to the sale, which lasted a whole week, to buy a piece of Burlington history or just to get a glimpse inside the soon-to-be-gone mansion that had been a mystery or completely unknown to most for many years.

In the spring of 1958, Frank Wells's dream home was demolished. A new residential street, Summit Ridge, was put in. It ran from Cliff Street to where the mansion had stood. The portions of the estate on South Willard and Summit Streets were also converted into residential lots. When all was said and done, the property became the site of forty-four high-end homes on an estate that was formerly occupied by two people and two servants.

OAKLEDGE

The Oakledge property has a long and storied place in Burlington history. The first recorded owner was Abram Brinsmaid, who ran a jewelry store in Burlington dating back to before 1800. A part of the property, known as the shipyard lot, was the location of a shipyard where numerous lake canal boats and two lake steamers were built, including the 258-foot *Oakes Ames*, at that point the largest steamboat built on Lake Champlain. In 1870, the land passed to Lawrence Barnes, another man notable in Burlington history. Barnes conveyed the land to Dr. William Seward Webb in 1883. Dr. Webb and his wife, Lila, built a twenty-four-room mansion as well as barns and numerous other outbuildings on the property, and in 1884, they first occupied the Burlington property. They retained their New York City residence, a mansion at 680 Fifth Avenue, where they still spent considerable time.

It seems odd to say, but the 245-acre Oakledge property with its twenty-four-room mansion soon proved inadequate. But it is important to keep in

Oakledge Manor was built in 1883 as the residence of Dr. William Seward Webb and Lila Vanderbilt Webb. It would later be expanded and become the public resort Oakledge Manor and later the Cliffside Country Club. It was destroyed in a controlled burn by the City of Burlington. *Author's collection.*

mind that Lila was a Vanderbilt, the money was unlimited and Oakledge did indeed seem modest compared to the estate at Shelburne Farms, where the Webbs relocated after living a few years at Oakledge.

Oakledge remained in the Webb family for a number of years after Dr. and Mrs. Webb vacated it. It was used for other purposes, including as a place for musicians to stay while performing at Shelburne Farms.

While it may not have measured up to Shelburne Farms, the Oakledge property was gorgeous in its own right. With nearly a mile of lake frontage, including an excellent beach, spectacular views and rocky bluffs, the property was highly desirable. So, in 1929, a group of local businessmen purchased Oakledge with the intention of converting it into a resort.

The resort was named Oakledge Manor, and the main house remained the focus, with guest rooms and the large dining room. But eight private cottages were constructed on the grounds, all named for U.S. presidents, for guests who desired a bit more privacy. A wide variety of recreational activities were available to guests, from water sports to roller skating. After a slow start due to its opening right as the Great Depression was descending on America, Oakledge Manor established itself as a successful venture.

Oakledge Manor operated as a summer resort until 1960. At that point, it was acquired by the General Electric Athletic Association (GEAA). By then, the property had been reduced to sixty-two acres. GE was the largest private employer in Burlington at the time, and 90 percent of its employees belonged to the GEAA, an employee organization designed to provide recreational activities for GE workers. The GEAA changed the name of the resort to Cliffside.

GEAA operated Cliffside until 1971. After much wrangling over the price, the City of Burlington finally acquired the property with the intention of converting it to a public park. On July 19, 1971, the twenty-four-room mansion built by the Webbs in 1883, which had been greatly expanded in the resort years, was intentionally set on fire by the Burlington Fire Department and destroyed in a controlled burn. A picnic shelter now stands roughly where the Webb mansion once stood.

THE JOEL GATES HOUSE

Joel Gates was a partner in Gates and Kilburn, a furniture manufacturer founded in 1858 on the Burlington waterfront. On the death of Gates's brother Stephen, the firm came to be known as Kilburn and Gates. In 1869, it built a huge new manufacturing complex, with the main building spanning an entire city block on Kilburn Street. The structure still exists and was reported to be the largest furniture factory in the United States when it was built.

Gates would later split with his partner, Cheney Kilburn, and convert his furniture factory into a cotton mill.

As a result of his business activities, Gates became a very wealthy man, and as had come to be the practice of the city's wealthy elite, he had a grand home built. The home stood at 381 Main Street, the gateway street to Burlington. It was high enough up the hill to have a nice lake view. The twenty-room home featured eight bathrooms. The style is hard to pin down architecturally, featuring a variety of elements, but Colonial Revival with Georgian elements seems to best describe it. The house had a lot going on, from its rounded front bays to a beautiful cupola-style belvedere on top. A good case can be made that the Joel Gates house is among the most beautiful wood-frame homes ever constructed in Burlington.

Gates lived here until his death in 1909. His widow lived to be ninety-seven, and she was still living at the home when she died in 1937. After that, the house was a private residence, a boardinghouse, a dormitory at the University of Vermont and a UVM sorority house and then was cut up into eight apartments.

The residence of Joel Gates, partner in the Kilburn and Gates furniture business and later owner of the two Chace cotton mills in Burlington. This showplace stood on a prominent lot on upper Main Street, one of many showplace homes along that stretch that gave visitors their first impression of Burlington. *Author's collection.*

The house was lost in a fire on a bitter cold March day in 1993. The blaze was thought to have started as a result of squirrels chewing on electrical wiring.

THE HENRY WELLS HOUSE

Henry Wells was one of the four Wells brothers who were partners in the firm Wells Richardson discussed previously. All four of them built mansions in Burlington, and Henry's was at 368 Main Street, almost directly across the street from Joel Gates's house.

Built in 1889, the structure was one of many showcase homes on Main Street, a main thoroughfare for travelers entering the city via carriages and,

The Henry Wells home stood nearly across the street from the Joel Gates house. Henry, like others in the Wells family, made a fortune from the Wells Richardson patent medicine firm. Later taken over by the Kappa Sigma fraternity, the residence burned in 1975. *Author's collection.*

later, automobiles. The homes of the street were a testament to the wealth and taste of the city's elite merchant class.

The seventeen-room Victorian is not spectacular in any respect. It was a very nice, large home on a prime city lot. But compared to the homes of his brothers and father and his nephew Frank, the Henry Wells residence could almost be called modest. Certainly it was historic as the residence of one of the partners in Wells Richardson, one of the most important companies in Burlington's history.

Henry did not enjoy good health and died at sixty-two in Miami. His widow died in 1937. She had remarried twice, and on her death the home went to her third husband, but he died the following year. The house then went to the late Mrs. Wells's niece. She immediately sold the building to Kappa Sigma, a University of Vermont fraternity.

The home was ideally suited to the fraternity. It had a bowling alley in the basement and plenty of room for the frat brothers, who had to eat in the basement of their previous chapter house. The spacious home and a caretaker's cottage in the back provided ample sleeping quarters.

Dozens of Burlington's historic homes have housed UVM fraternities and sororities for over 125 years. Many of these fine old homes have taken a beating from partying, carousing and other activities associated with Greek life. But, remarkably, no historic residence had been lost to fire while housing a fraternity or sorority. That lucky streak came to an end in March 1975, when Kappa Sigma was destroyed in a fire that killed one of the fraternity brothers. The fire was not caused by the activities of any members of Kappa Sigma but was found to be caused by faulty wiring.

4

SCHOOLS

Back in the 1860s, Burlington had more than sixteen grammar schools. Even with a small population of around eight thousand, the city needed that many schools because there was no public transport and schools needed to be within reasonable walking distance. Most of the schools were in the central core of the city, with a few in the rural areas, such as the north end and in what would later become the city of South Burlington (in 1865). Burlington's neighborhood schools were small wooden buildings of one story and usually topped with a small bell tower.

The city started a long economic boom after the Civil War, largely generated by Burlington's favorable location on Lake Champlain. It was ideally situated for lake and rail transport between Canada and the major northeastern cities to the south. The lumber business, the main driver of Burlington's economic growth, was very labor-intensive. So the mills and factories of the city attracted more and more workers, and the population of school-age children exploded as a result.

POMEROY AND THE OLD BURLINGTON HIGH SCHOOL

In response to this, in 1871, the city opened its first high school worthy of the name, a large stone and brick Second Empire building on the corner of College and South Willard. The high school was three stories, with a mansard roof capping the building. A square bell tower rose over the front entrance, and it was capped by a curved roof surmounted by a

The Burlington High School building at the corner of South Willard and College Streets is seen shortly after its completion in 1871. When this building was torn down in 1965 and replaced by apartments, it ended a public school presence on this corner that had lasted 150 years. *Courtesy of Vermont Historical Society.*

large ornamental iron crown, which was very typical of French Second Empire towers at that time. Two years later, the city constructed its first two substantial grammar school buildings, the Pomeroy School in the city's north end and the original Adams School on the south side of town. Both were two-story brick structures, forty-five by seventy-eight feet and topped by bell towers. Each could accommodate one hundred students. The city was justifiably proud of these new buildings, but they would soon prove to be inadequate to accommodate the city's rapidly growing population of school-age children.

The city muddled along for years without increasing school capacity. The two new grammar schools were immediately well over capacity, as were all of the remaining older schools. Year after year, the number of students increased, and the city kept making do by renting space or adding more students to already overcrowded schools. The situation was becoming an embarrassment to the city, typified by one citizen's complaint that many horses in the city were in better quarters than the schoolchildren of Burlington. Something had to be done.

THE CONVERSE SCHOOL

What followed was a golden half decade for the construction of schools in the city of Burlington. In 1893, Burlington constructed what has to be regarded as the most magnificent school building ever erected in the city. The Converse School, on the corner of Pine and Cherry Streets in the heart of the city, dwarfed the 1870s schools in both size and splendor. Burlington hired the Findlay, Ohio architecture firm Kramer and Zoll to design the building, and a contractor from that city got the contract to construct the new school.

A spectacular building was erected that the city was justifiably proud of. A portrait of the new school graced the inside cover of the 1893 city report, and five pages were devoted to a very detailed description of every aspect of the structure. The photo shows it right after completion. Adding to the list of prideful aspects of the building was the fact that it was built almost entirely using local materials. The school was named in honor of

The Converse Grammar School, designed by Kramer and Zoll of Findlay, Ohio, was the most magnificent public school ever built in Burlington. It was demolished in 1966 as part of urban renewal. *Courtesy of Champlain College Special Collections.*

John K. Converse, an early pastor at Burlington's First Congregational Church and a longtime superintendent of Burlington schools. His son John H. Converse made a fortune in Philadelphia and was a notable benefactor of Burlington. The Converse dormitory at UVM is his most memorable legacy.

The dominant feature of the Converse School was a massive circular stone bell tower. It was complemented by four huge ornate chimneys, two on each side of the building. Above the second-floor balcony over the main entrance, the words *Converse School* were carved in stone. Heavy stone arched entrances are the hallmarks of the Richardson Romanesque style, which probably best describes this building, the exterior of which was constructed of Ohio sandstone and local brick.

The Converse School replaced a small former church that had been converted to a school by the city and was known as the Pine Street School.

IRA ALLEN AND THAYER SCHOOLS

In 1894, two more excellent school buildings went up in Burlington: the Ira Allen School on Colchester Avenue and the S.W. Thayer School on North Avenue. W.L. Kramer of the firm Kramer and Zoll designed both, and the schools were constructed simultaneously by another Findlay, Ohio contractor, George Kratt. While much smaller and less ornate than

the Converse School, the Ira Allen School was a charming structure of brick with stone decorative elements and topped by a tall brick bell tower with a gracefully curving roof. Thayer School, though unmistakably from the same design, was much smaller, only one story versus two for Ira Allen. This was mainly due to the fact that there still were not many school-age children that far out on North Avenue at the time.

The 1894 Ira Allen School on Colchester Avenue was built simultaneously with the Thayer School on North Avenue. Ira Allen was demolished for a modern replacement. Thayer is the only school built during Burlington's golden half decade (1890–95) that still stands. *Burlington City Report.*

LAWRENCE BARNES SCHOOL

In 1898, the city topped off a half decade of more than making up for past foot-dragging with the opening of the Lawrence Barnes School on the corner of Murray and North Streets. The school was clearly a Richardsonian Romanesque design of heavy brownstone and brick with terra-cotta decorative elements. Like Converse, a large stone bell tower topped off the building. Lawrence Barnes replaced a much smaller, antiquated wooden school that had sat on that corner for many years.

These schools were quite unlike any that had been built before in Burlington. Rather than basic structures to provide shelter during learning, these were statement schools. They said that the City of Burlington valued education. They were buildings that any city would have been proud of, and they said that the education of the children of the city was an important priority.

Of these schools, only Thayer, the least of the four, is still standing. As time went by, the schools came to be seen as inefficient. These 1890s buildings had a lot of what would come to be seen as wasted space—large central halls, very high ceilings and so forth. The bell towers proved to be a problem, as they were open to the elements, causing leaks that eventually penetrated the roofs into the rooms below. Years before they were demolished, the bell towers of Converse, Barnes and Ira Allen as well as the 1871 high school building were removed to prevent further damage. Ornate stone and brick structures are very expensive to maintain, so a lot of the needed maintenance was put off. The schools got to the point where officials deemed them too far gone to save. New, efficient and modern was pretty universally seen as better than old, historic and ornate.

Lawrence Barnes was the first to go. It was demolished in 1956, replaced by a modern school building, also named for Lawrence Barnes and erected next to the old school. Converse had some defenders, as it was seen to be an important building architecturally. The advocates for demolition made the arguments about inefficiency and deterioration mentioned earlier. But the fate of Converse was ultimately decided by its location. It stood in a zone targeted for total clearance by the city as part of the federal urban renewal program. Everything on the block where Converse stood had to go. The school was too large and heavy to be moved, so it went under the wrecking ball in 1966. Ira Allen persisted a bit longer. After the city stopped using it as a grammar school, it was used by another school for about fifteen years. It was demolished in 1974.

The 1895 Lawrence Barnes School stood on the corner of North and Murray Streets. It was built in the Romanesque style, echoing H.H. Richardson's Burlington masterpiece, UVM's Billings Library, built ten years earlier. *UVM Silver Special Collections.*

The 1873 Pomeroy School was nearly doubled in capacity when a huge addition was put on in 1899, but eventually age got to the structure, and it was vacated by the city in 1939. It was used by several groups until 1945, when it was leased to the Catholic Diocese of Burlington. The diocese carried out needed repairs and used Pomeroy to accommodate overflow student population from its nearby Cathedral High School. This ended in 1959, when the diocese opened the new Rice Memorial High School. That same year, the eighty-eight-year-old Pomeroy School was finally torn down.

The 1873 Pomeroy School is seen after it was nearly doubled in size in 1899. One of the earliest two-story brick schools in the city, Pomeroy served as a public school until 1939. Other uses extended its life until it was finally torn down after eighty-eight years of service. *Burlington City Report.*

The 1871 Adams School was demolished in 1898, and a new school, also named the Adams School, was constructed on the South Union Street site. It is still standing but is no longer a school. The 1871 high school building had been replaced by the new Edmunds High School building (still standing) in 1900. But the old high school was used for a variety of other purposes until 1965, when it too was razed. The building that was torn down looked nothing like the 1871 high school building, as both the bell tower and the entire third-floor mansard roof had been removed years earlier.

No discussion of lost Burlington schools would be complete without including two prominent Catholic schools that were built in the downtown core of the city. The demographics of the city had changed much over the years, and waves of immigrants, mostly Catholic, had moved to the city to work in the various mills and factories in town. For a number of years, there had been a school associated with St. Joseph's Church on Allen Street, and one for parishioners of the Cathedral of the Immaculate Conception (also known as St. Mary's) on the corner of Cherry and St. Paul Streets. St. Joseph's was Burlington's "French church," while Cathedral was largely the parish of the Irish and Italians who inhabited the neighborhoods around the Cathedral of the Immaculate Conception, the 1867 Cathedral Church of Burlington.

CATHEDRAL GRAMMAR SCHOOL

To accommodate the ever-growing numbers of school-age Catholic children, the old St. Mary's school was replaced by the new Cathedral Grammar School, which opened in 1901. It stood diagonally across St. Paul Street from the Cathedral Church, on the corner of Cherry and St. Paul. It was an impressive brick structure, with two huge projecting gables flanking the building's dominant feature, a tall, rectangular brick bell tower that was surmounted by a lofty stone belfry. This spire was the tallest on any school or church ever built in Burlington. Gothic arched windows and entrances in the front completed the look of the immense school, which quickly became the largest school in terms of enrollment in the city.

The fate of Cathedral Grammar is intertwined with Cathedral High School, as explained in the following section.

Cathedral Grammar School is seen just before its demolition in 1959. The building served the Catholic students of Burlington for nearly sixty years. A parking lot now occupies its former location. *Courtesy of UVM Silver Special Collections.*

CATHEDRAL HIGH SCHOOL

For many years, the vast majority of schoolchildren did not go beyond elementary school. After eight years (or less) of grammar school, most kids went to work or just stopped going to school. High school was not something that was expected to be part of the lives of most kids growing up in the late 1800s in Burlington. That slowly began to change, but despite the longtime presence of Catholic grammar schools in the city and huge enrollment in those schools, there was still no Catholic high school in Burlington where the students from St. Joseph's and Cathedral grammar schools could continue their education in a Catholic institution. This was remedied when Cathedral High School opened in 1917. It was located just north of the Cathedral Church, on the corner of St. Paul and Pearl.

The school opening was a bit unusual, because the school began with only a freshman class. The following year it had freshman and sophomore classes, and so on, until it finally reached the full four classes in the fall of 1920. When the school opened, the United States was just entering the First World War. An ad for the new high school promised that German would not be taught within its walls and that military instruction would soon be added to the curriculum.

Unlike the public Edmunds High School, which opened in 1900 without a proper gymnasium to host basketball games, the new Cathedral High featured a full gym and bleachers in the basement. Edmunds and Cathedral Highs, along with many buildings of that period, featured basements that rose well above ground level. The result was an abundance of large windows on all sides, making the basement much brighter than one would expect. The Cathedral basement also featured other recreational amenities, including a two-lane bowling alley, one of the earliest in town, along with three pool tables and leather couches for those watching the bowlers.

The building was a classic Collegiate Gothic design, built of Indiana sandstone and brick, with numerous carved stone elements enhancing the already handsome building. The carvings were done by Alexander Milne of Boston, the same man who carved the capitals and moldings on the University of Vermont's Billings Library in 1885. Two projecting bays

Cathedral High School. *UVM Silver Special Collections.*

marked the front of the school, and eight stone pinnacles topped the bays. The main Gothic-style entrance was on Pearl Street, with the Latin words *Deo et Patria* ("God and Country") carved in stone over the entrance. Two smaller entrance doors were on the east and west sides of the building. These side entrances were to provide separate entrances for the boys and the girls.

Both Cathedral schools thrived for decades, and Cathedral became the crosstown rival of Burlington High School (Edmunds). But in 1959, the Catholic diocese opened Rice Memorial, a larger, modern high school in South Burlington, replacing Cathedral High School. That same year, the diocese closed the 1901 Cathedral Grammar School and transferred its students to the old Cathedral High School building. A few months after the grammar school was vacated, the school building was demolished, and its site became a parking lot.

The Cathedral High School building continued to function as the home of Cathedral Grammar School until 1971, when the diocese decided to close Cathedral Grammar. The cathedral parish used the building as a parish center for a few years, but in 1976, the old Cathedral High School was also demolished. Historic preservation still had a long way to go.

ST. ANTHONY'S SCHOOL

Once the trolley line of the Burlington Traction Company extended down Pine Street to Flynn Avenue (then known as Park Avenue), the growth of that formerly remote area in the south end of town was guaranteed. A new, large, sixteen-block housing development known as the Ferguson-Scarff Addition promised to bring businesses and residents to the area. The Queen City Cotton Mill opened on Lakeside Avenue in 1894 and employed hundreds of workers, quickly filling the homes of the Lakeside neighborhood. Most of the workers in these new plants were Catholic. These developments caused the Catholic diocese to erect a church called St. Anthony's on the corner of Pine Street and Park Avenue in 1902.

Because St. Anthony's was far removed from the Catholic schools then available in Burlington, it was decided to build a school in the south end, associated with St. Anthony's Church. The new school, located on a lot immediately south of the church, was in the Collegiate Gothic style, as were many of the area's Catholic school buildings, such as Cathedral High, Trinity College and Michael's College.

St. Anthony's School opened twenty years after St. Anthony's Church was built on the corner of Pine Street and Flynn Avenue. Both were built in response to rapid growth of the Catholic population in the south end of Burlington. *Author's collection.*

The new school opened in 1921. The building also contained a convent to house the nuns who came to teach at the school. While enrollment at St. Anthony's was always much smaller than at Cathedral and Nazareth in the center of the city, it was healthy, with 365 students in 1934. While the opening of the more centrally located Christ the King School in 1940 no doubt affected St. Anthony's enrollment, it was still strong enough that it was pushing up against a self-imposed limit of 35 students per class in the early 1960s.

But just a few years later, in 1970, enrollment had dropped to 190. The administration and the diocese decided that the school was not sustainable and elected to close it in 1971. The nuns moved out of the convent, and the building served as a daycare center for a few years before being demolished in 1980. The site is now green space.

THE EPISCOPAL INSTITUTE

On November 21, 1832, the Reverend John Henry Hopkins was consecrated in New York City as the first Episcopal bishop of Burlington. Three weeks later, he moved his fifteen-member family into a large brick home that he purchased in Burlington.

The home had been built by William Chase Harrington in 1799. The home was located on lower Church Street (now 272 Church Street). Bishop Hopkins purchased the building from Harrington's heirs and, in 1833, designed two wings that were added on the north and south sides of the structure. The north wing would house a chapel, while a school would be located in the south wing. The school would be a seminary and serve to educate future generations of Episcopal priests, starting with the three theology students who moved into the house along with Hopkins' family.

That first attempt to establish an institute for theological training ended in failure. The bishop, his wife and their thirteen children struggled along in near poverty during their years on lower Church Street.

But Bishop Hopkins had fallen in love with a tract of land in a remote section of the city. The land sat on a bluff and had been cleared years ago by loggers. From that site, spectacular views were available of the lake and mountains to the west as well as the city of Burlington to the south.

The bishop leased and later purchased one hundred acres on what would come to be called Rock Point. With the help of his thirteen children, Bishop Hopkins erected a new home of his own design. The stone for the building was quarried on-site. Hopkins had earlier published a treatise on designing Gothic churches, so he knew a bit about architecture. The home was completed and occupied by the Hopkins family in December 1841.

The Hopkins family lived at Rock Point for the next fifty years. They were committed to transforming their farm into a center for Episcopal education and a home for future bishops.

So, in 1844, the building on lower Church Street was sold to Reverend John K. Converse. He converted it into a female seminary, which ran until 1880. In 1921, the Home for Aged Women on the corner of Bank and St. Paul Streets purchased the old seminary building, and it became the new location of the facility, renamed the Converse Home in 1954 and so called to this day.

Back to Rock Point. In 1857, the dream of an Episcopal institute was revived, and construction of a large structure in the Gothic style was initiated. As with the house, stone from Rock Point was used in the

The Vermont Episcopal Institute is seen in winter. It featured a school for boys that was joined by a school for girls when Bishop Hopkins Hall opened in 1889. The Rock Point School, now coed, remains in operation in the Hopkins Hall building. *Author's collection.*

construction. Completed in 1860, the building, formally known as the Vermont Episcopal Institute, housed the seminary and a boys' school. The stone tower of the institute bears a great resemblance to the bell tower of St. Paul's Cathedral in Burlington, a building that Bishop Hopkins would have had great familiarity with. The tower housed the stained-glass windows of the institute's chapel, but the very top of the tower served a more utilitarian purpose. It concealed the institute's water tank, which was elevated to provide water pressure.

Sitting on a cleared promontory, the Vermont Episcopal Institute was visible for many miles. It can be seen in the distance in old photos taken from the waterfront area of the city.

The Civil War broke out right after the school opened, and military training at the school was instituted. For most of its existence, the school featured a corps of cadets known as the Rock Point Cadets. An armory was located next to the institute building, where the cadets drilled during the long Vermont winters.

Attendance at the boys' school gradually declined, and the school closed in 1899. The building sat vacant for three decades, but finally, in 1929, it came back into use as a spot for church activities and conferences.

On the day before Easter in 1979, the 120-year-old building was destroyed by fire. Bishop Hopkins Hall, which opened in 1889 as a school for girls, and the residence of the Episcopal bishop of Burlington still occupy the grounds. The old girls' school is now known as the Rock Point School and is still in operation, now open to both boys and girls.

The road leading from North Avenue to the old Hopkins property still bears the name Institute Road, after the lost Vermont Episcopal Institute.

5

CHURCHES

Like everything else in the early days, Burlington's churches were all
located within a very small area of the city's downtown core. The
city's oldest church is undoubtedly its best known. The 1816 Unitarian
Church still stands at the top of Church Street, which takes its name from
the historic church at its northern end. This church has come to symbolize
Burlington and is likely the most photographed feature of the Queen City.

But it is joined by several other historic churches downtown. The First
Baptist Church, First Methodist and First Congregational all date to the
Civil War or before. In a city not known for tall buildings, for many years, the
spires of Burlington's churches constituted the only semblance of a skyline
the city possessed.

Yet while the city retains these beautiful, historic churches, Burlington has
also suffered severe losses of sacred buildings. Two historic cathedrals and
two smaller churches have been lost over the years.

TWO CATHEDRALS

Of all the losses reflected in this volume, there is no doubt that the losses
of the two Burlington cathedrals were the most shocking and saddening for
the people of the city. They had stood on adjacent blocks on St. Paul Street
for over a century. They had been a part of so many generations that there
was a feeling that they would always be there. The structures were not only

imposing and magnificent but also beautiful. Their loss devasted not only the parishioners of the two churches but also the public at large. The loss of these two churches within a year of each other still resonates today.

These cathedrals were a vital part of the streetscape and of the architectural heritage of the city. When they were removed, not only were they gone, but the very streets that they stood on disappeared as well, altering that area in ways that are impossible to describe in words. You really had to have seen the area before these churches vanished to realize the immensity of what this loss did to the city.

Both churches were built at a time when the construction of an Old World–style stone Gothic cathedral was still possible in the United States. By the time there were lost, replacing them as they were was just not possible.

ST. PAUL'S CATHEDRAL

St. Paul's was the cathedral church for the Episcopal diocese of Burlington. The original St. Paul's Cathedral was completed in 1832 on the street that still bears its name. The design was by Burlington architect Ammi Young. Young was from New Hampshire but had moved to Burlington and opened an architecture office. He would later become the supervising architect for the U.S. Treasury Department and design government buildings across the country in that role. Two of his designs still stand in Burlington, the Wheeler House on the UVM campus and the Follett House, which still overlooks Burlington Harbor. His other two Burlington designs, St. Paul's and the old Custom House, are gone. He also designed a beautiful Congregational church in Winooski, just across the river from Burlington. That building is also gone.

St. Paul's stood on the corner of St. Paul and Bank Street. Young's church was a fairly basic rectangular design with a square bell tower in front topped by four pinnacles. In 1850, the cathedral was expanded. A transept was added, giving St. Paul's the cruciform layout that one would expect of a cathedral. In 1881, a chapel of matching design, connected to the church, was added. This was a gift from one of Burlington's greatest benefactors, John Purple Howard, who had made a fortune in the hotel business in New York City.

The interiors of both the church and chapel were done in a dazzling array of woodwork featuring columns, hammer beams, paneling and wainscotting, all done in dark chestnut. A fine stone rectory, which would not have been

The interior of the 1832 St. Paul's Cathedral is seen decorated for Christmas in the late 1800s. *UVM Silver Special Collections.*

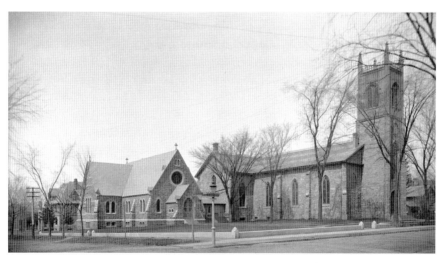

St. Paul's Episcopal Cathedral, with its chapel and rectory, are seen at the corner of St. Paul and Bank Streets. This corner no longer exists. *Courtesy of UVM Silver Special collections.*

out of place among the grand homes on Willard Street, completed the complex. The sprawling church and associated buildings covered most of the city block they sat on.

St. Paul's chapel suffered a severe fire in 1910 that nearly destroyed the parish house (chapel) but left the main church intact. The chapel was gutted, but the low walls were able to be reused. A firm from Brandon, Vermont, rebuilt the parish house in six months, replicating the stonework and the interior woodwork to closely approximate the original.

St. Paul's was an important part of the Burlington community and a downtown landmark. But during the afternoon of February 15, 1971, everything changed. Three men at a service station across the street noticed that St. Paul's was on fire. Despite the fact that the Burlington Fire Department's main station was just a couple of blocks away, the firemen could do little to slow the progress of the blaze. With the church full of varnished wood well over a century old, the fire quickly became a raging inferno. The streams from the fire hoses seemed to have no effect at all. Once the main church had been gutted, the flames moved into the adjoining parish house and consumed that as well. Only the rectory, which stood a bit apart and unconnected from the church, survived unscathed.

The loss of St. Paul's was a shock to the community. It had stood there for generations and was irreplaceable. Unlike in 1910, when the burned parish hall was replicated in six months, by 1971, a building like St. Paul's couldn't be put up anymore.

The shell of St. Paul's was not knocked down immediately, because the site became the subject of negotiations between the parish and out-of-state developers. The firms were planning to redevelop blocks just to the west of the St. Paul's site. They had acquired the narrow portion of the block just north of St. Paul's to give them a corridor connecting their development to Church Street, Burlington's main shopping street. The rest of the block, occupied by the historic and still thriving St. Paul's, was rightly thought to be unobtainable. But the fire changed all of that, and the St. Paul's site came into play, as a sale to the developers became a viable option.

Negotiations dragged on for months, and all the while the charred shell of St. Paul's stood silent on the corner of Bank and St. Paul, a sad reminder of what once had been. But the two parties finally reached an agreement in the form of a land swap. The developers acquired the St. Paul's site, and the parish was given a large parcel on the corner of Battery and Pearl, which would become the site of a new, modern St. Paul's Cathedral. The burned-out remains of the old cathedral were finally cleared, but one casualty of the land swap was the old St. Paul's rectory. The fine old stone residence, though undamaged, was of no use to the developers and only stood in the way of their plans, so it was ultimately demolished as well.

The cause of the fire was said to be accidental, but Burlington endured a plague of arson fires in the 1970s, and many locals to this day believe the fire was deliberately set.

THE CATHEDRAL OF THE IMMACULATE CONCEPTION

As more Catholic immigrants came into Burlington, the Church acted to minister to the needs of their growing flock in the Queen City. A historically important move was the assignment of Louis DeGoesbriand as the first bishop of Burlington. He was from Brittany, France, and had been assigned to the United States, initially going to Cleveland, Ohio. But in 1853 he came to Burlington as bishop and began the work of building the Church in Vermont.

That meant recruiting new priests; establishing parishes; and erecting churches, orphanages, convents and other Catholic institutions. DeGoesbriand was a tireless builder, and he had the added advantage of a large reservoir of personal funds to aid him in his projects. The son of a wealthy French family, he inherited a fortune of $250,000, a massive amount of money at that time. But he was not at all interested in the comforts such wealth could provide. Instead, he often used his own money to buy land for church projects or to provide funds needed during the course of building. When he died in 1899 he had $2.12 in his bank account.

By 1862, the bishop had decided that it was time for the Diocese of Burlington to have a proper cathedral church. He enlisted architect Patrick Keely of New York City to design a cathedral for Burlington. Keely immigrated to America from Ireland in 1842 and had quickly become engaged in designing churches in large American cities. His cathedrals still stand in many major cities of the eastern United States. Keely had designed numerous cathedrals by the time he was hired to create one for Burlington, which would be one of his smaller cathedrals. Bishop DeGoesbriand knew Keely from his days as the pastor of a church in Toledo, Ohio. Keely had designed a church for him there.

In May 1862, the cornerstone was laid for St. Patrick's chapel, which would be attached to the northern end of the cathedral itself. Construction of the small chapel was swift, and it would house services until the much larger cathedral itself was finished.

The interior of the Patrick Keely–designed Cathedral of the Immaculate Conception shows the highly decorative main altar and two side altars. *Author's collection*.

In September 1863, the cornerstone of the cathedral was laid. Keely's design was of a classic cruciform Gothic church, with a large rose window above the front entrance on Cherry Street. The design featured many other arched stained-glass windows, buttresses, second-floor galleries and a large bell tower, and everything was built of cut stone. The stone was locally sourced from Willard's quarry in Burlington. All of the stained-glass windows were imported from France. Kelly was well known for his highly ornamented interiors, even in some of his plainer churches. The Burlington cathedral would be no exception, replete with statues, columns, sub altars, pews and galleries, all featuring ornately carved wood and stone. The main altar would be a feast for the eyes.

But the work proceeded slowly due to the short construction season of northern Vermont and the aggravating factor of manpower shortages caused by the Civil War. Parishioners were doing a lot of the preliminary work of dressing the stone and other tasks, and with so many men away, the construction timetable was considerably extended.

But finally, on September 30, 1867, the first High Mass was held in the new church, celebrated by Bishop DeGoesbriand, who had just returned from a foreign tour. The splendor on the interior was remarked on by several dignitaries attending the event.

A large number of stained-glass windows were the subject of considerable comment. The triple east windows were donated by a Protestant woman from Bennington who had been a longtime supporter of Bishop DeGoesbriand's charities.

The cathedral was formally consecrated in a daylong ceremony on December 8, 1867, the feast of the Immaculate Conception. Previously referred to as St. Mary's, the cathedral became formally known as the Cathedral of the Immaculate Conception, although many continued to refer to it as St. Mary's.

But although consecrated, the building was not completely finished. The large bell tower and a smaller tower had temporary caps placed on

The Cathedral of the Immaculate Conception, often called St. Mary's in earlier times, is pictured in 1954. Constructed of red stone from Willard's quarry on Shelburne Road, the cathedral was the centerpiece of several Catholic institutions at the top of St. Paul Street. *Library of Congress.*

top to protect them from the weather. These capped towers would not be completed until that work was included as part of a 1904 refurbishing of the cathedral. A large gilt statue of Mary was installed at the top of the bell tower. She would look out over Burlington for nearly seventy years.

Like St. Paul's, the end came by fire. On March 13, 1972, fire broke out in the Catholic cathedral. As with the fire in the Episcopal church, the interior wood furnishings and framework provided fuel for a fire that soon was out of control. The entire church was consumed, including St. Patrick's chapel and a large rectory building next door that had once served as the residence of the bishop of Burlington. The cause was soon determined to be arson. The fire was set by a former Cathedral altar boy.

One block down St. Paul Street, the charred shell of St. Paul's was still standing thirteen months after it had been destroyed by fire. For three months the burned-out ruins of both former glorious Burlington cathedrals stood a stone's throw from each other, presenting a desolate and incredibly sad scene to passersby.

The final fate of St. Paul's had been delayed because of the land-swap negotiations previously mentioned. When that deal was finally settled, parishioners gathered at the old Episcopal cathedral one last time for a ceremony to secularize the church, which had been consecrated in 1832. A few days later, wreckers came in to take down what remained of the 140-year-old-church. They also demolished the undamaged rectory, as the property was now entirely owned by private developers, who planned to build a shopping mall through the site.

The walls of the Cathedral of the Immaculate Conception then stood alone for another eight months. Officials said that the building was unsafe. Its walls were much higher than those of St. Paul's and were in danger of collapse. Nonetheless, the demolition was delayed as various plans were floated for saving a part of the building. Those centered mainly on St. Patrick's chapel, whose walls were much lower and relatively sound. But in the end, it was decided to take down the chapel along with the main cathedral and the rectory. This was done a couple weeks before Christmas 1972.

Unlike St. Paul's, a new Catholic cathedral would rise on the site of the one lost to fire. But the era of building Gothic cathedrals in Burlington, Vermont, had long passed. Inadequate insurance, along with the fact that people to do the skilled work required to put up such a structure were just not around anymore, meant that a very different-looking cathedral would take the place of Patrick Keely's masterpiece. The new cathedral was very modern, with its steep sheet-metal roof dominating the look of the structure. Although embraced by some architecture writers, longtime parishioners compared it in their minds to what had been there before, and it's safe to say that the new cathedral was generally unloved.

An overall downward trend in church attendance in the ensuing years, along with the ability of cathedral parishioners to attend mass in the beautiful St. Joseph's Church that stood just a few blocks away, led to a dramatic decline in the number of people attending services at the cathedral. In 2018, the diocese announced that the church would be closed and deconsecrated, becoming a secular space. St. Joseph's, which had been a co-cathedral for a number of years, would become the Cathedral Church of the Diocese of Burlington.

As this is being written, an application has been filed with the city to demolish the replacement cathedral. If that were to happen, it would bring to an end nearly two centuries of Catholic presence on the top blocks of St. Paul Street in the heart of the city, a presence that at its height included two large schools, a huge rectory, a chapel and, of course, the church building itself.

THE BEREAN BAPTIST CHURCH / WCTU TEMPLE

The Berean Baptists are an offshoot of the Baptist Church, and in the late 1800s, there were enough Bereans in Burlington for them to be able to construct a small church.

The church was really more of a chapel, and it stood for many years on the northwest corner of Pearl Street and North Winooski Avenue, one of the busiest corners in Burlington. It was built in 1885 by the Berean Baptists in a style that is a bit reminiscent of something you would see in an alpine village.

But for most of the building's existence, the little church on the corner was the Burlington temple of the Woman's Christian Temperance Union. The WCTU was founded in Ohio in 1873, and the Burlington branch quickly followed a year later. The group's main cause was the prohibition of alcohol (which was ultimately achieved), but it also crusaded against tobacco and advocated for many causes related to the rights of women and children. For example, it was ten members of the Burlington WCTU who founded the Home for Friendless Women (later the Elizabeth Lund Home) in 1890. Elizabeth Lund was the longtime president of the WCTU in Burlington. Helping unmarried mothers was just one of many causes that she and her WCTU colleagues worked tirelessly on. Her husband, Dr. William Lund, was a medical doctor who assisted the WCTU ladies in their many endeavors. When he died a few years after his wife passed away, he left his estate to the Home for Friendless Women to honor her. It was renamed the Elizabeth Lund Home in her memory.

In their early years, the WCTU met at various downtown locations, mainly members' homes. As its membership grew, they started meeting in rooms at

Although the Berean Baptist Church on the corner of Pearl Street and Winooski Avenue has been torn down, several exact copies of this small church can be found within an hour's drive of the city. *Courtesy of UVM Silver Special Collections.*

the YMCA building, and eventually, in 1896, they purchased the relatively new Berean Baptist Church building. The Burlington chapter became one of the few WCTU chapters with its own building, which they referred to as the WCTU Temple. The only change they made to the exterior of the building was the installation of a panel above the four windows facing Pearl Street on which were displayed various short biblical quotations in support of positions they were advocating. One early photo of the temple displays the quote "Woe unto him that giveth his neighbour drink" (Habakkuk 2:15).

Prohibition on a national scale came and went, but the local WCTU soldiered on (it still exists nationally). But as older members died, and with its signature issue dead and buried, the Burlington WCTU started to wither. Eventually, the temple was leased to the Church of the Nazarene. But by the early 1950s, the WCTU wanted to sell the building, preferably to that church. But the Church of the Nazarene lacked the funds for the purchase, so the little church was sold to the Gulf Oil Company, which demolished the structure and built a gas station on the site. The gas station was later demolished, and that corner is now occupied by a parking lot and a very nondescript, one-story brick addition to the building next door.

There are at least two other churches in the Burlington area that are exact copies of the lost WCTU Temple. One is the former Methodist church on route 15 in Essex Junction. Another is the United Methodist church on Route 7 in Ferrisburg.

ST. JOSEPH'S ON THE HILL

Early Burlington was nearly 100 percent Protestant, but that would change as waves of immigrants started moving to the city to work in the many mills and factories there. Although many nationalities were represented, by far the largest two groups were the French Canadians and the Irish, both overwhelmingly Catholic.

To serve this new frontier of Catholicism in North America, two pioneering priests, one French and one Irish, were dispatched to what would be best described as a mission. Their charge was to build up the Church in Vermont to serve the many adherents to the faith who were flocking to the Burlington area.

The earliest Catholic services in Burlington were held in the courthouse building, which stood between Church Street and Court House Square. But the goal of both priests was to build a church for their parishioners.

In 1830, a prominent citizen of early Burlington, Archibald Hyde, deeded five acres of land where St. Joseph's cemetery now stands. Hyde would later convert to Catholicism. A church named St. Mary's was built on this land, but it burned in 1838. A chapel for French worshippers was also built on this property, but it was sold after the French priest, Father Ance, left the area in 1843.

A new St. Mary's was built in the heart of downtown Burlington on St. Paul Street. This was commonly referred to as the Irish church, with Father Jeremiah O'Callaghan as pastor. The church was shared with the French, with two sermons being delivered, one in English and one in French.

But St. Mary's was not a good option for the French for many reasons. Unlike the previous St. Mary's, the new one was located far from Winooski, the home of many of the area's French Canadian Catholics. The fact that many of the French did not speak English, along with their feeling of being second-class citizens by virtue of not having their own church, combined to spur the desire for the construction of a French church.

So the effort was organized, and funds were raised, allowing for construction to begin on the first St. Joseph's Church on August 22, 1850. It was located at the end of North Prospect Street, across from the Fern Hill estate. The land it stood on was elevated considerably, leading to it quickly becoming known as St. Joseph's on the Hill. There were sweeping views from St. Joseph's, especially from the steeple. Several 1870s stereoviews taken from the steeple are captioned "view from the French Church." The new church was roofed over in time for Christmas Mass to be celebrated there, and the church was consecrated on June 1, 1851.

The original St. Joseph's Church was known as St. Joseph's on the Hill. After it was replaced by a much larger church on Allen Street, it was dismantled and the materials used to construct St. Anthony's in Burlington's south end. *From* The History of St. Joseph's Parish.

St. Joseph's on the Hill served the area's French Catholic population for several decades, but the continued growth of that population soon rendered the 1850 church inadequate. Winooski's Catholics opened their own large new church, St. Francis Xavier, in 1871. But even with Winooski's Catholics eliminated from the equation, it was obvious that Burlington's French Catholics also needed a new place of worship. On September 5, 1883, work was begun on a new, much larger St. Joseph's Church, which still stands on Allen Street in Burlington. St. Joseph's on the Hill was now excess property, its main function eliminated. It continued to stand, used for various services.

By the end of the nineteenth century, Burlington was expanding beyond the old center of the city. Growth in the south end was spurred by the opening of the Queen City Cotton Mill, along with the development of a sixteen-block area known as the Ferguson Scarff Addition. As a result, the Diocese of Burlington decided to construct a new church, to be called St. Anthony's, at the corner of Pine Street and Flynn Avenue (then called Park Avenue).

The materials for the new church came from the old St. Joseph's on the Hill, which was dismantled, with the materials being transported to the south end and used to build St. Anthony's. In addition to the brick and wood, four stained-glass windows that had been installed in the old church in 1880 were taken out and reinstalled in St. Anthony's in exactly the same location that they had occupied in the old church. Likewise, a bell that had been installed in 1856 at St. Joseph's was placed in the belfry of St. Anthony's. So the new south end church bears a remarkable resemblance to the now gone St. Joseph's on the Hill. St. Anthony's did get a taller, more ornate steeple than the one that topped St. Joseph's, but that was unfortunately destroyed in a lightning strike in 1969.

6

CHARITABLE INSTITUTIONS

I n Burlington's early history, just about every charity was privately run and nearly always by women. The officers of the various charities were usually wives of prominent men in the community. But the founders of three of Burlington's greatest charities, the Mary Fletcher Hospital, the Home for Destitute Children and the Howard Relief Society, were all women who never married and who suffered from ill health. Two of the three had great fortunes. All three of the institutions live on today, although under other forms or names. The hospital is not covered here, because the original 1879 building still stands on Burlington's "hospital hill."

The phrase "Christian charity" applied literally to these early Burlington institutions, because Christianity was the driving force behind the founding of most of these charities, and Christian instruction was an important part of their program in most cases.

These institutions, though located in Burlington, accepted cases from all over the state and occasionally from other states.

THE LOUISA HOWARD MISSION HOUSE / HOWARD RELIEF BUILDING

Louisa Howard was the daughter of John Howard, who for many years ran a hotel in Burlington. Her brothers John Purple Howard and Daniel D. Howard became extremely wealthy in the hotel business in New York City.

It's a bit unclear how Louisa came into her money, but it was likely inherited from her father. In the tradition of her brother John, one of the greatest benefactors ever in the city, she used her good fortune throughout her life to assist the less fortunate members of the Burlington community.

She went by the name of Louisa, even though her given name was Hannah Louisa Howard. She suffered from poor health most of her life and never married, devoting all of her energies and resources to charitable and religious causes. A prominent Burlington landmark, the Louisa Howard mortuary chapel still stands in Lakeview cemetery, but the other important building endowed by Miss Howard has been lost.

Louisa Howard died in 1886. Among her last words were, "Let no money be wasted on my funeral, save it for the poor." Her considerable estate was left in varying amounts to dozens of relatives, along with numerous religious and charitable causes in the city. But by far the greatest portion, $30,000, was designated to be used to build a permanent home for the Howard Relief Society, said home to be called the Louisa Howard Mission House.

The Howard Relief Society had been renting space for years in the Exchange Block on the corner of Main and Church Streets. The new building would ensure a permanent home for the relief organization. In addition to the funds for the building, Howard left substantial funds for the continuing support of the relief organization. Work on the building commenced soon after the will was finalized.

The resulting handsome structure was dedicated in 1888. It's a bit hard to pin down the building to one style. The three-story brick structure featured a mansard roof in the French Second Empire style, but projecting bays topped by turret roofs break up the mansard roofline and give the building strong elements of a chateau style. It stood on the corner of Pearl and Clarke Streets, across Clarke from the 1816 Unitarian Church. Louisa Howard's building was a worthy complement to that historic Burlington church and to the magnificent Richardson building, which still stands across Pearl Street.

The building housed various entities involved in public service over the years. It remained in the possession of the successor organizations to the Howard Relief Society, which always kept the Howard name alive through various name changes. The current iteration is called simply the Howard Center. Eventually, the 1888 building no longer was suitable for the needs of its owners, and in 1964, those owners, then called the Howard Family Service Center, decided to sell the building. It was put on the market for $35,000.

The Louisa Howard Mission House gave a beautiful home to the Howard Relief Society, founded by Louisa Howard. The charity lives on today as the Howard Center. The 1888 building was purchased by the Abernethy's department store in 1964 and torn down for a parking lot. *Courtesy of UVM Silver Special Collections.*

It was purchased by Abernethy's Department store. Abernethy's was a longtime Church Street retailer that traced its origin to 1848. It occupied the 1895 building at the top of Church Street known as the Richardson. Abernethy's and the Richardson were both Burlington icons. But by the 1960s, the retail scene had undergone dramatic change. Burlington's Church Street had been the center of retail commerce in the city for well over a century. From the horse-and-buggy era, through the time of the trolley cars and into the automotive age, Church Street was where people went for just about every type of shopping.

But the rise of car culture was changing the way people shopped. The dominance of downtown was being severely challenged by several suburban shopping centers with their acres of free parking. Parking spaces downtown were limited, and none of them were free. Several longtime Church Street retailers had either gone out of business or moved out to the shopping centers.

Against this backdrop, the proprietors of Abernethy's saw the land occupied by the 1888 Howard Mission as a way to provide parking for their customers and to help stave off the pressure from their suburban competitors. So in 1964, the Howard Relief building was purchased by Abernethy's for $35,000 with the intent of knocking it down and creating a parking lot across the street from the store.

Shortly after the sale, the building was razed. Historic preservation was not really something people thought of back then. The sale and demise of the Louisa Howard Mission House was reported briefly and in a very matter-of-fact manner. There was not a word mentioned in contemporary reporting about the historic nature of the building, its beauty or its architectural value. Most people felt that if you owned a property you had the right to do what you wanted with it.

The acquisition of the parking lot may have helped Abernethy's to forestall the inevitable, but the venerable downtown department store did close in 1982. The site of the lost Howard Relief building remains a parking lot to this day.

THE HOME FOR DESTITUTE CHILDREN

In the early history of Burlington, there were no government entities other than the poorhouse to provide for those who could not take care of themselves. Since the poorhouse was not intended for children, the question of how to care for orphans and other children whose parents could not take care of them became more pressing as the population of the city grew.

As more workers migrated into the city to work at the many mills and factories, the number of children of the working poor greatly increased. For reasons such as "intemperance" (drinking), poverty, neglect and disability, more and more families just could not adequately take care of some or all of their children.

Burlington's Catholic bishop Louis DeGoesbriand established an orphanage on Pearl Street in Burlington in 1854, but it only partially met the needs of the community's children. There was still a lot of anti-Catholic feeling at that time, and it's likely that many parents would not have wanted to turn their children over to a Catholic-run facility. So many needy cases literally depended on the kindness of strangers. For example, Miss Lucia Wheeler was taking care of four young girls at her small brick home on Main Street (the current 449 Main). She was the daughter of the Reverend John Wheeler, former president of the University of Vermont, whose large home stood across Main Street from Lucia's.

The number of girls under her care increased to seven, but Wheeler, who was an invalid most of her adult life, realized that her strength was not adequate and her home too small to accommodate the number of children needing care. So the first Home for Destitute Children was set up in a brick building at the corner of Winooski Avenue and what was then called Maiden Lane (now the top of North Union Street). But this building, which is now gone, was just a stopgap, so in 1866, Wheeler and six other women organized a corporation to be known as the Home for Destitute Children. It was originally founded as the Home for Destitute Girls, but over time, boys were admitted as well. As soon as the existence of this new refuge became known, applications started coming in from across the state, and the ladies knew that a large facility would be required to meet the need. The purpose of the facility was to house and care for children, to meet all of their needs and to try to place as many as possible in proper permanent homes.

The ladies focused on the Marine Hospital on Shelburne Road. This large facility had been built by the federal government in 1859. It was part of a program run by the U.S. Treasury Department to build hospitals for mariners along the coasts and inland waterways of the country. The Burlington facility, intended for Lake Champlain mariners, was never much used for that purpose. It was pressed into service as a hospital for soldiers wounded during the Civil War, but when that conflict ended, the Marine Hospital became excess government property. It was offered at public auction, and the Home for Destitute Children was able to the buy the building, which had cost the government $25,000, for $5,000. Prominent local businessmen, who would have been likely bidders under normal circumstances, agreed among themselves not to bid against the ladies running the Home for Destitute Children, thus enabling them to get it at a bargain price.

The building accommodated forty children and served well for ten years. In 1875, the original hospital was renovated and substantially expanded using private donations. The resulting structure looked nothing like the Marine Hospital, as a mansard roof was added, along with a large wing. It increased the capacity to one hundred persons. Several wealthy benefactors, chiefly John N. Pomeroy and John Purple Howard, contributed greatly to the Children's Home, as it came to be known. Their gifts enabled the home to become debt-free and self-sustaining. Howard's gift was particularly important. In 1881, he deeded his huge Howard Opera House, which still stands on the corner of Bank and Church Streets, to the home. The opera house was one of the finest in New England, and profits from the many events held there now went to support the Children's Home. By 1889, the

Although this was the third location of the Home for Destitute Children, this renovated and expanded Marine Hospital was the charity's first institutional-sized building that came close to addressing the needs of the city's children. This structure was destroyed in a fire in 1893. *Vermont Historical Society.*

The rebuilt campus and main buildings of the Children's Home are seen in 1912. The home sat on the corner of Shelburne Road and Home Avenue, which takes its name from the facility. After providing a refuge for Burlington's needy children for a century, the Children's Home buildings were torn down in the early 1960s and replaced with a shopping center. *UVM Silver Special Collections.*

value of the buildings and endowment of the Children's Home ranked third in Burlington, behind only the University of Vermont and the Mary Fletcher Hospital. The generosity of many people had put the home on a sound financial footing.

But on the night of May 1, 1893, the Home for Destitute Children was destroyed by fire. As it was located on a large lot far from the city center, there were no hydrants in the area. Water pumped from nearby Potash Brook was totally inadequate to fight the fire.

The home was underinsured. The insurance money available was used to build new boys' and girls' dormitories and a kitchen and dining facility. An appeal raised enough from donors to build a separate building to house the school, hospital and other services provided to the children. The new buildings were spaced well apart, cottage style, so that in the event of another fire, the entire home would not be lost, as happened in 1893. This new version of the Home for Destitute Children would stand on the corner of Shelburne Road and Home Avenue for nearly seventy years. The adjacent street, Home Avenue, takes its name from the Children's Home.

Finally, by the early 1960s, Burlington had expanded to the point where the formerly remote lot housing the home had become desirable commercial real estate. The rise of the automobile, and the fact that the Children's Home stood next to the entrance to the new interstate highway being built, meant that the time of the Home for Destitute Children on that property was coming to an end. The site was purchased by a developer, who razed the entire Children's Home complex and built a shopping center with a huge paved parking lot in front. The Children's Home, after a century on that corner, moved a bit west to a smaller, modern facility on Pine Street.

THE BURLINGTON POOR HOUSE

Like most sizable communities, for many years Burlington maintained a poorhouse as the last resort for people who had no place to go. A government official, the Overseer of the Poor, supervised the poorhouse, which for many years was the only direct aid to the needy of any sort provided by the city government. Private charities did everything they could to assist the needy, but a few always ended up at the poorhouse, often the disabled or the elderly. Foreign-born individuals were also disproportionally represented at the Burlington Poor House. It was a place you did not want to end up in.

Typically, people stayed at the poorhouse for less than a year. The exception was the elderly. When an aged person ended up at the facility, it was because they had no one. They usually ended up spending the rest of their days there.

After being located in the city center for a number of years, the poorhouse was eventually moved away from town when Burlington purchased a sixty-acre farm with extensive lake frontage. The facility was located well down Shelburne Road, over a mile south of the city center. The former poorhouse now became the poor farm, where residents were expected to help with the chores to produce much of the food they consumed. When South Burlington separated from Burlington in 1865, Burlington's poorhouse stood in the town of South Burlington.

By 1902, the prime lakefront of the poor farm parcel, which included a beach and striking views, attracted the attention of George H. Allen of New York City. He purchased the entire property for $9,200. He intended to develop the parcel into the Allenwood Estate (later a resort), giving Burlington a year to relocate its poor farm to a new location.

This brick structure was built in 1903 in Burlington's north end to house the city's poor. This was the last of the poorhouses in Burlington, closing in 1954. *From Burlington City Report.*

The city looked in the other direction and, in 1903, relocated its poor farm to the far northern end of the city on what was then called Goodrich Road (now Ethan Allen Parkway). Part of the former Nash farm became the new poor farm. As with the previous location, the poor farm was located in an isolated spot far from the city center. A total of $10,000 was allocated for the construction of a two-story brick poorhouse on the site.

The new poorhouse would remain in use until the 1950s. By that time, reforms such as Social Security and housing for the elderly had rendered poorhouses unnecessary. Burlington finally closed its facility in 1954, and the 1903 building was torn down. The office of Overseer of the Poor disappeared from city government.

THE HOME FOR FRIENDLESS WOMEN

For many years, there was a powerful societal stigma against unwed motherhood. It created a terrible dilemma for the pregnant girls and women and their families. The father could marry the mother, of course, but then, when the baby came, people would do the math, and it would be obvious what had happened, so the stigma was not avoided in this way, just lessened somewhat.

In many cases, the girl was sent on some pretext to an out-of-the way town where she could have the baby. Then the baby was generally put up for adoption; after a while, the mother returned home, and no one was the wiser. The stigma was avoided. That at least was the hope. There are no numbers as to how often this happened, of course, because it was done in secret. But this seems to have been the course sought by quite a few families facing this situation. There were facilities in various parts of the state that made a business of accommodating girls who were "sent away." If a family couldn't afford that option, there really weren't any alternatives. The woman had the baby locally and endured the stigma.

But the women from the Burlington chapter of the Woman's Christian Temperance Union (WCTU) resolved to do something about it. The WCTU's main mission was the elimination of alcohol, but it advocated for and supported many women's causes as well. In 1890, ten members of the Burlington WCTU drew up a charter for a new residential agency to provide for socially abused and rejected women. It would "provide for poor and friendless women, destitute of the means of support, and wherein such women may enjoy the comforts and advantages of a quiet, peaceful

Christian home." The home would be called the Home for Friendless Women (HFW). On November 4, 1890, the state legislature approved the charter but provided no money. Despite being located in Burlington, the services provided by the HFW were available to women from across the state and beyond. For years, the HFW was the only home for unwed mothers in Vermont and New Hampshire.

Here is some background on the Christian part of the story. Burlington in 1890 was a very different place. Christianity, especially Protestant Christianity, was a very important part of the culture, especially the charitable culture. It was a time when the front page of Saturday's paper featured synopses of the sermons to be preached at every church the following day, as well as hymn lists. Pastors of Protestant churches were highly respected and well-known members of society, and every congregation provided a grand home for the leader of their church. Virtually every leader of Burlington's business community was a pillar of his church, nearly always Protestant. Their wives were the organizers of Burlington's charitable community. This was at a time when few government programs existed; those that did, like the poor farms, were pretty awful.

So the WCTU came at this from a Christian perspective. While going to great lengths to help unwed mothers, the ladies of the WTCU saw them as "fallen women."

Since they had no funding, the HFW's organizing meeting elected officers and put together a fundraising plan. Mrs. M.E. Bell, president of the Burlington WCTU, was elected the first president of the HFW.

After a little over a year, the organization had raised just over $13,000. The state legislature refused Bell's request for $10,000. On March 30, 1893, the group used nearly all of its funds to purchase the former Frederick Weed estate at 346 Shelburne Road, which included a large Victorian mansion and substantial grounds. On April 12, 1893, the HFW opened there.

You did not have to be an unwed mother to use the HFW. The first resident was a destitute woman who was provided care for two months. HFW records indicate that she was not a "fallen woman." The first baby was born to the third resident, a woman who had been abandoned by her husband. Her baby was born on September 12, 1893, and was delivered by Dr. William Lund. Dr. Lund's wife, Elizabeth, was a devoted member of the WCTU, joining it shortly after the Burlington chapter was formed and remaining a member for twenty-seven years, including many years as president, until she died in 1917.

Doctors and nurses from Mary Fletcher Hospital served at the home as needed. Residents were preached to at Sunday services, as the ladies of the

The former mansion of Judge Frederick Weed on Shelburne Road would become the Home for Friendless Women in 1893. The charity, later renamed the Elizabeth Lund Home, occupied the building for seventy-seven years. It was demolished when the Lund Home opened a new facility in 1970. *Author's collection.*

WTCU hoped to get them to turn to the Lord to get back on the right path. Significantly, the HFW accepted only women pregnant with their first child. Second pregnancies would not be admitted.

For many of the early years, the HFW struggled financially. At one point, it nearly lost the house, having to sell a substantial part of the land to prevent that from happening. That would change in 1924, when Dr. Lund died. He and Elizabeth had no children, and he left a bequest of $115,000, nearly his entire estate, to the HFW in honor of his late wife. The will was contested for other reasons, but shortly after it was settled, the HFW was renamed the Elizabeth Lund Home. That was pretty much the end of what had been constant financial worries for the home.

The opening of the HFW did nothing to reduce the stigma against unwed motherhood. Only time would do that, but many decades would pass before that happened. Untold numbers of girls and women continued to be "sent away" to have their children. A Richford, Vermont sanitarium ran ads in

Burlington papers advertising this service in the 1920s. Other institutions advertised similar services.

In 1948, the Lund Home reached a milestone, as the two thousandth baby was born in its care. In 1966, a campaign to raise $750,000 for a new building was launched. The state legislature kicked in $311,000, a nice change from its lack of support at the start. In 1969, a new building opened on Glen Road, and the old Weed mansion was demolished in 1970.

7

SANITARIUMS

The climate and surroundings of Burlington were thought to be healthful. Crisp, clean air, clean water, quiet, abundant trees, parks and open spaces and so forth. In the minds of many, this was a perfect atmosphere for rest and rehabilitation for all types of ills. This resulted in the establishment of numerous sanitariums within the city. In the early twentieth century, at least six sanitariums were operating in Burlington.

GREEN MOUNTAIN SANITARIUM

The Green Mountain Sanitarium occupied the former home of Henry P. Hickok. Hickok was born in 1804 and was prominent in the early years of Burlington as a businessman, mainly in lumber and banking. He was president of the Merchants Bank for over thirty years after rescuing it from ruin. He was also very supportive of local institutions, including the University of Vermont, city schools and the Congregational church.

In 1861, he constructed a large mansion on the northeast corner of Pearl and North Union Streets. His home was a large, three-story brick building with a mansard roof. It was surmounted by a tall tower incorporating a belvedere and a widow's walk on top. The home was elaborately trimmed and surrounded by parklike grounds on the large corner lot. A substantial carriage house behind the residence built in a style matching the home completed the estate. The result was one of the showplace homes of Burlington.

This 1861 mansion, built by Henry P. Hickok, became Burlington's first sanitarium after his death in 1878. After a long run as a sanitarium under several doctors, the building at the corner of Pearl and North Union Streets was sold to the First National grocery chain. It demolished the old mansion and built a supermarket on the site. *Author's collection.*

Hickok died in 1878, and his son-in-law Dr. A.J. Willard was the first to use the home as a sanitarium, specializing in the treatment of nervous disorders. In 1888, he built his own building, specially designed as a sanitarium at the corner of North Prospect and Loomis. The building, the so-called Willard Nervine Home, still stands at that location.

In 1895, the Hickok residence was purchased by Dr. W.R. Prime, who established his practice there under the name of Dr. Prime's Sanitarium, later to be known as Green Mountain Sanitarium. Dr. Prime focused on physical ailments more than had Dr. Willard.

Dr. Prime was succeeded in 1913 by Dr. Thomas Hays, who bought the building and ran it as the Green Mountain Sanitarium until it closed in 1941. Dr. Hays offered treatments for an extensive array of ailments using the latest technologies and techniques.

The First National Supermarket chain had run small grocery stores in Burlington for many years. But now it was looking to close all of those small outlets and build one large supermarket downtown. It first explored acquiring space adjacent to Abernethy's department store just off Church

Street, Burlington's main shopping street. That did not work out, and First National started looking at properties a few blocks from downtown. The Green Mountain Sanitarium building became available, and First National decided to locate its supermarket there, two blocks from downtown. The site was attractive, because it was near Church Street and had ample space for the supermarket building and a good-sized parking lot. So, in May 1941, the building and its carriage house were demolished and the First National supermarket was built on the lot. One interesting note was that trees, shrubbery and even the lawn from the residence were transplanted to the grounds of City Hall Park and Memorial Auditorium before the demolition.

SPARHAWK SANITARIUM

Unlike the Green Mountain Sanitarium, the Sparhawk Sanitarium was purpose-built for that use. The structure was completed in 1887 and stood on the northeast corner of Bank and St. Paul Streets, less than one block from Church Street, the heart of the city's downtown. The three-story stone and brick main building could have passed for a mansion. Although not particularly ornamental, the substantial structure featured a large, rounded porch topped by a windowed turret on its west side.

Run by Dr. G.E.E. Sparhawk, MD, this sanitarium specialized in baths of various sorts. Advertisements touted the availability of Electro-Vapor, Turkish, Roman, Russian, sulfur and medicated baths. In addition to the usual claims to cure nervous disorders, Dr. Sparhawk's baths were said to "renovate and restore one's entire system." They would "cleanse the skin, equalize the distribution of vital fluids, remove the causes of disease, beautify the complexion, tone and quiet the nervous system, promote digestion, cure dyspepsia, neuralgia, rheumatism, paralysis, colds, catarrh, and diseases of the liver and kidneys." Such claims were not unusual in the unregulated heyday of patent medicines.

Dr. Sparhawk's baths and promises found plenty of willing customers. People came from the local area and from far away to partake in the curative baths offered at the sanitarium. In addition to the baths, many came to attempt to seek treatment for alcohol abuse. The facility offered an early version of rehab, so to speak. Patients who came from afar would stay for weeks or months.

Sparhawk performed surgery there, and the sanitarium was also the scene of numerous births. The relatively new Mary Fletcher Hospital still did not

The Sparhawk Sanitarium differed from Burlington's other sanitariums in that it was located in the heart of downtown, on the corner of Cherry and St. Paul Streets. After a long run as a sanitarium and then as the Odd Fellows Lodge, the property was sold to the Burlington Federal Savings Bank, which demolished the buildings and built a modern steel and glass headquarters on the corner. *Author's collection.*

accept maternity cases at this point, and the sanitarium was an option for those who could pay and did not want their baby to be born at home.

In 1896, the original Turkish bathhouse, which was in a separate building resembling a carriage house, was enlarged dramatically. A huge, four-story bathhouse building was constructed to keep up with the demand. As the bustle of downtown grew, the location of the sanitarium in the heart of the city became a disadvantage. An early twentieth-century photo shows a "Quiet Hospital Zone" sign in front of the building.

The years passed, and Dr. Sparhawk died in 1906. His son Sam Sparhawk, also a doctor, took over the operation of the sanitarium after his father passed away. When the second Dr. Sparhawk died unexpectedly in 1925, there was no one to keep the business going. The sanitarium property was put on the market, and in 1926, it was purchased by the Burlington chapter of the Odd Fellows. They constructed a new lodge hall on the northern portion of the large lot and rented out the old sanitarium buildings as apartments and offices.

In 1958, the Odd Fellows sold the property at the corner of Bank and St. Paul, including the lodge hall and old sanitarium buildings, to the Burlington Federal Savings Bank. The bank demolished all of the buildings on its newly acquired property and constructed a modern glass and steel bank building on the site. It still stands there today.

LAKEVIEW SANITARIUM

Unlike all of the other sanitariums in Burlington, the Lakeview Sanitarium was located far from the city center. It stood on a large plot of land on North Avenue, just north of the St. Joseph's Orphan Asylum building, which still stands. The main building had thirty-four rooms, and there were numerous outbuildings, including barns, greenhouses and cottages. Lakeview, as the name implies, had a spectacular view of Lake Champlain from its grounds. The site was originally the estate of Sion E. Howard, a member of the very prosperous Howard family so well known in Burlington history. Howard died in 1866, and his estate on North Avenue was offered up for subdivision,

Built as a sanitarium and located far from the city center, Lakeview Sanitarium offered a pastoral setting to its clients. When its time as a sanitarium ended, it served as the Don Bosco School for boys for a number of years. *Author's collection.*

but it wasn't until 1881 that UVM graduate Dr. John Clark returned to Burlington, purchased the entire estate and converted it into a sanitarium.

Ads for Lakeview indicate that it specialized in treatment of "nervous and mild mental diseases." Alcohol and drug habits were specifically mentioned. The pastoral setting of the sanitarium was a big selling point. Guests could stay in separate cottages in a parklike setting and enjoy the gardens and the view and even mingle with sheep and other farm animals.

Given the advantage it enjoyed due to its location, the sanitarium prospered for many years. It finally closed in 1945, and the land and buildings were acquired by the Roman Catholic diocese of Burlington. The diocese turned the property over to Vermont Catholic Charities, which renovated the main building into a school for boys called Don Bosco School. It operated along the lines of the famous Boys Town in Nebraska. Vermont Catholic Charities moved into another building on the property as its new headquarters.

Don Bosco School closed in 1966. After a few years as a drug rehab center, in 1974, the 1880 Lakeview Sanitarium building was torn down as a fire hazard.

8

TRANSPORTATION

STEAMBOATS

Lake Champlain had been an important transportation artery for Native American tribes for uncounted years before Samuel de Champlain became the first European to enter the lake in 1609. When the first white settlers started to put down roots in Burlington and interior roads were still nearly nonexistent, the lake became the primary means of communication and commerce. Subject to the vagaries of the wind, travel via sailing vessel was undependable and usually slow. But that all changed in 1809, when the steamboat *Vermont* was launched at the foot of what is now King Street in Burlington.

The *Vermont* was the second steamboat in the world, after only Robert Fulton's revolutionary *Clermont*. When the *Vermont* set off on its maiden voyage to St. John's, Quebec, it started an era of steamboats on Lake Champlain that was to last 150 years, with Burlington the main port of call. Over that time, a total of twenty-nine different steamboats would ply the waters of the lake. Steamboats were a common sight coming and going from Burlington, along with numerous other ports of call in Vermont, New York and Quebec. Passengers were transported in high style, with later boats featuring elaborate stateroom halls with ornate wood and brass trim. Boats featured overnight staterooms and a fine restaurant with an extensive menu for those on longer voyages.

The steamboat *Vermont* is seen departing Burlington harbor around 1900. The vessel was the third to carry the name *Vermont* and was the largest steamer ever on the lake. Steamboats served passengers on Lake Champlain for 150 years. *Library of Congress.*

As time went on and the area's population grew, the size and speed of lake steamboats increased dramatically. The largest of all was the *Vermont III*, namesake of the boat that started it all. Launched in 1903 from Shelburne Shipyards, it was the next-to-last steamboat built on the lake. It was the longest, at 262 feet, and the fastest, capable of twenty-three knots. Contemporary reports agreed that it was also the most elaborate and beautiful Lake Champlain steamer ever.

The rise of the automobile, and particularly the opening of the Champlain Bridge across Lake Champlain at Crown Point in 1929, brought about the decline of the steamboat on the lake. Most passenger runs were cut, and steamers hung on mostly as car ferries or excursion boats. The *Vermont III* spent its last years on the lake tied up idle at Shelburne Shipyard.

Because vessels can reach tidewater only via the two narrow canals at the northern and southern ends of the lake, steamboats were too big to exit the lake. So Lake Champlain's steamboats were built at various points on the lake, and after their service was over, the lake was their final resting place. But the final three steamers built, *Chateaugay* (1888), *Vermont III* (1903) and *Ticonderoga* (1906), did end up leaving the lake one way or another.

Chateaugay was stripped of everything but its hull, which was then cut into sections and shipped by rail to Lake Winnipesaukee, in New Hampshire, where it was welded back together as the hull of the tour boat *Mount*

Washington. The *Vermont III* was stripped of its entire superstructure, allowing it to pass through the Champlain Canal. It was converted to a diesel freighter operating up and down the East Coast. After service there for a number of years, it sank during one of its runs. But the *Ticonderoga* was saved, first by a group led by Ralph Nading Hill, which raised funds to save it from being sold and likely scrapped and got it back on the water for a few last years as an excursion boat. Electra Webb, founder of the Shelburne Museum, then had the old steamer taken out of the lake in 1953 and transported overland on improvised railroad tracks to its final resting place at the museum.

CANAL BOATS

With the 1823 opening of the Champlain Canal connecting Lake Champlain with the Hudson River, waterborne commerce to and from Burlington increased dramatically. The Chambly Canal to the north, completed a few years later, provided access by water to the major markets and suppliers in the United States and Canada.

This began the canal boat era on Lake Champlain. Large, boxy craft, they were designed to maximize the loads they could carry and have been called the eighteen-wheelers of their day. They were towed on the canals by horses, mules or steam tugs. Once out on the lake, those equipped for sailing raised their masts and sailed their way to Burlington. The majority, lacking the capability to sail, were towed to Burlington by tugboats.

They brought all manner of goods with them, but the dominant cargo was logs and lumber to feed the numerous insatiable mills and factories along Burlington's waterfront. Several of the larger waterfront mills were churning out over fifty million board feet of finished lumber annually. So the number of boat trips required to keep the mills running was prodigious. Like steamboats, canal boats were a common sight at the Burlington docks and traveling up and down the lake.

By 1833, 233 canal boats were registered on the lake or the canals. That number increased to 450 ten years later. Between 1870 and 1915, 1,800 different boats worked the lake and the canals.

The coming of the railroad to Burlington in 1849 presented a challenge to the monopoly canal boats had enjoyed to that point. The railroad had several great advantages over the canal boats. They were much faster and could pull right up to the mills via sidings to be unloaded or loaded. But their greatest advantage was that trains could run twelve months a year, while Burlington's long winters limited canal boat trips to seven or eight months. With each passing year, canal boats became less of a factor until, by the turn of the century, they were a rare sight.

THE RAILROAD DEPOT

Although the first train arrived in Burlington in 1849, the city did not have a proper depot for rail passengers until the late 1860s, when the city's Union Station opened, so called because this depot served both railroads running through Burlington, the Vermont Central (later called the Central Vermont) and the Burlington and Rutland (later the Rutland Railroad). Unlike most passenger depots, which tend to be located in the heart of the city, Burlington's was located on the waterfront, alongside the freight yards of the railroads and the factories and mills of the lumber industry. It was hardly a dazzling welcome to the Queen City. A short coach ride (later via trolley) was needed to reach the city's hotels and other accommodations.

The brick depot featured two large flat-topped towers flanking the main entrance, four smaller corner towers of similar style and five ventilators on top with cupola-style roof treatments identical to the corner towers. The

The 1860s Union Station served both the Vermont Central and the Burlington and Rutland lines as their Burlington depot. Eventually, the station was replaced by the 1916 Union Station, which still stands. *Courtesy of UVM Silver Special Collections.*

ventilators, designed to vent smoke out of the train shed's roof, were an unusual feature. As originally built, the station featured several arched openings on either end, but these were later replaced by one large opening. For a brief time, a lighted beacon for mariners was installed on one of the station's two main towers.

One odd aspect of this depot is that the president of the Vermont Central Railroad, John Gregory Smith, insisted that the front entrance face the lake. There was a lot of disagreement about this, but Smith, powerful politically and a former governor, was able to get his way. As a result, photos of the depot usually show it from the side. The depot's main entrance can only be seen in photos taken from the lake, and existing photos from that side are either too far away or have something blocking the view of the depot, usually a steamboat. Consequently, the main entrance to the Burlington depot can only be fully seen in Stoner's 1877 *Bird's Eye View of Burlington*, which is a drawing.

This depot stood until it was replaced by another Union Station in 1916, at which point the old depot was demolished.

HORSE CARS AND TROLLEYS

In the early days of the city, two vital elements of city life—schools and grocery stores—were located within walking distance of everyone. Every neighborhood had its own school and one or more neighborhood grocers. Everything else was located downtown, on Church Street and its adjoining blocks. There was no mass transit, so if you didn't have a horse and carriage (or wagon), you walked anywhere you needed to be. Getting about was even more difficult during Burlington's long winters, when a sleigh or "your own two feet" were the only options.

So the first murmurings of any form of public transportation reached many eager ears. The first solid indication that something was at least in the works was the issuance of a charter to the Winooski and Burlington Horse Railroad in 1872. But putting together such a system was complicated and expensive. It meant laying railroad tracks on all planned routes, acquiring conveyances and horses and hiring staff. It all took capital and was seen by many as a risky investment. Did Burlington really have the population to support such a venture?

Years passed with nothing being done. It was thirteen years before the long-awaited horse railroad made its debut, on November 16, 1885. The first trip was a cause for celebration all along the route from City Hall to just over the bridge in Winooski.

Horse cars were slow; the horses proceeded at a walk. But you could sit down during the trip and were sheltered from the elements. Passengers could take in the scenery, knit or read a book to pass the time. It certainly beat walking, but not by a whole lot in terms of time.

But the time of the horse cars in Burlington was short, and in 1893, they were replaced by the electrified trolley cars of the Burlington Traction Company. The trolleys were much faster than the horse cars, were roomier and had plows for the winter months. The speedier and more comfortable trolleys did heavy business, resulting in extensions of the existing lines. The system eventually extended to Essex Junction, Ethan Allen Park, Queen City Park and Flynn Avenue. Ads for businesses, apartments and homes for sale often mentioned "close to the cars" or "close to the trolley line" as a feature that would make their property more enticing. Everyone recognized the value added by the trolley lines.

A trolley car of the Burlington Traction Company is seen heading down Church Street in the early 1900s. At the left are several horse-drawn carts, including an ice wagon. To the right, an early automobile can be seen. *Library of Congress.*

As the automobile era dawned, trolleys faced a competitor in the form of buses. The bus had several advantages over the trolley, the most obvious being that it was not limited to the few streets where rails had been laid down. Bus routes could be easily adjusted to meet changing circumstances. Buses were more comfortable, with the internal combustion engine providing heat not available in an electric trolley car. By the 1920s, everyone realized that buses were the future.

The last trip of a Burlington trolley car was on Sunday, August 4, 1929. Buses, which had been running in the city for some time, took over entirely after that last ride. Burlington gained some national notoriety by a ceremonial burning of one of its trolley cars. The burning took place at the intersection of Main and St. Paul Streets and attracted a huge crowd. Newsreel cameras filmed the event, and it was seen by millions in theaters across the country. The other trolleys were scrapped, bringing down the curtain on the era of the trolleys, a time many look back on wistfully, even though they were born well after trolleys stopped running.

9

CLUBS

THREE YACHT CLUBHOUSES

The Lake Champlain Yacht Club (LCYC) was founded in 1887. It was organized by the city's wealthy elite, whose names—Wells, Hickok, Ballard, Woodbury, Smalley, Whiting and Woodhouse—will be familiar to those interested in Burlington history. Initial membership was about 200, with 169 being city residents and other members coming from points up and down the lake and even beyond. The canals at the northern and southern ends of the lake enabled people from as far away as New York City and Montreal to become members. It was anticipated that membership would swell to 400 once the new clubhouse was completed.

Yachting was an activity engaged in by many members of Burlington's upper class, which is not surprising given the city's location on Lake Champlain, one of the best bodies of water for sailing in the country. This was also a time when members of the elite class belonged to many social clubs, and the LCYC clubhouse was where summer parties and cotillions could be held for members. It also featured regattas and other sailing competitions that one would expect from a yacht club.

The clubhouse was completed in 1888, and it was a worthy home base for the lake's yachtsmen. The large building featured a wide veranda on three sides of the ground floor. The second-floor interior space was surrounded by walls of windows on all four sides, affording views in all directions. A

The original 1888 Lake Champlain Yacht Club is seen with a steamboat tied up at its dock. The building burned in 1901. This is now the site of the Burlington Community Boathouse. *Vermont Historical Society*.

veranda also ran around all four sides of the second floor. The rooftop had a large area similar to a widow's walk for even better views to be had from the facility. The building was topped by a flagpole in the form of a mast complete with yardarm. The clubhouse was located at the former steamboat pier at the foot of College Street. The steamboat dock had moved south to the foot of King Street in 1880.

The clubhouse was a bit of an anomaly on Burlington's waterfront when it was built, as the waterfront was entirely taken up with industry. If you were standing on the veranda and looking east, you would see nothing but mills and factories and their associated chimneys belching smoke, along with acres of lumber stacked all over the waterfront. Trains and canal boats would be coming and going all day, loading or discharging cargoes. And hundreds of workers would be scurrying about in the course of their employ with the many waterfront firms. All of this was within a stone's throw of the LCYC clubhouse. But if you looked in any other direction, especially to the west, you would have some of the most spectacular views available to any city in the United States.

The yachts belonging to club members came in all sizes, and while most were sailing vessels, "steam yachts" were growing in popularity. The largest yacht of all was the *Elfrida*, belonging to Dr. William Seward Webb. Dr. Webb had married into one of the wealthiest families in America, the Vanderbilts, and everything he had, from his huge estate at Shelburne Farms to his private railroad car and *Elfrida*, was on a scale to make just about any other local version of it seem humble in comparison. The black-hulled *Elfrida* was 117 feet long, double masted and equipped with a steam engine as well. When it made the trip from Delaware, where it was built, it sailed around New England and up the St. Lawrence River, coming into Lake Champlain via the Chambly Canal. It was the longest vessel ever to transit that canal.

Elfrida was normally berthed at Dr. Webb's private dock at Shelburne, but it was a common sight off Burlington, as the city sits on the lake's widest point, nearly twelve miles across. The broad lake was more in keeping with an oceangoing yacht like *Elfrida* than Shelburne Bay, where its home dock was located. In 1889, Dr. Webb was named commodore of the LCYC and *Elfrida* its flagship.

With the coming of the Spanish-American War in 1898, *Elfrida* became the property of the U.S. Navy, whose records show that it was purchased from Dr. Webb for $50,000. A plaque at Shelburne Farms commemorates Dr. Webb's donation of the yacht to the navy, so perhaps he forgave the $50,000 price that had been agreed on.

The second clubhouse of the Lake Champlain Yacht Club had an even shorter life than its predecessor. It burned after ten years on the waterfront at the foot of College Street. *Author's collection.*

Whatever the case, *Elfrida* left Lake Champlain, but it was soon replaced by another *Elfrida*, this version sporting a white hull but otherwise very similar to its predecessor. The white *Elfrida* was a footnote to history; it transported Vice President Theodore Roosevelt back to Burlington from Isle LaMotte on receipt of the news that President William McKinley had been shot in Buffalo. A few weeks after that happened, the 1888 clubhouse was destroyed by fire, in November 1901.

It was quickly replaced by a second clubhouse, which was very nice but quite a bit smaller and less impressive than the original. That clubhouse didn't even last as long as its short-lived predecessor; it too was destroyed by fire, in 1911. A third clubhouse was built on the site in 1913. Although it incorporated the wraparound verandas of the original clubhouse, overall it was the least impressive of the three. That third clubhouse remained the home of the LCYC until the club left Burlington in 1936 for Shelburne Bay, as Burlington's waterfront became derelict with the decline of the city's lumber industry, the source of so much prosperity over the decades.

The last clubhouse served as a ferry terminal for a few years and was then abandoned. Burlington mayor John J. Burns made the cleanup of the lakefront one of his main priorities. Nonetheless, the deteriorating former clubhouse was not removed until 1944, when it was finally dismantled and the lumber salvaged.

THE ETHAN ALLEN CLUB

Another longtime social club in Burlington was the Ethan Allen Club. Its origins go back to the time before the city had a paid fire department and relied on volunteer fire companies. These companies were social organizations as much as they were effective firefighting groups. There were at least half a dozen of them in Burlington at any given time. Every prominent member of the Burlington community belonged to one. The upper floors of their firehouses were outfitted as club rooms, with leather couches, fireplaces and billiard tables. The ground floor was reserved for the fire apparatus. The volunteer fire companies could be counted on to participate in every parade held in the city, marching in their handsome uniforms along with their shiny fire wagons. Competitions among fire companies were also regular events, with companies racing to achieve the best time performing various firefighting activities, such getting a wagon to a fixed point and getting water pumping. Road races were also held, with members of several companies pulling their apparatus behind them in a race to the finish line. These competitions often pitted Burlington companies against those of other cities as far away as Albany and Boston, with ornate belts as the prizes. A company from Burlington even won the national fire race one year in Chicago. The company's prize was a new fire wagon and a championship belt of solid silver that weighed three pounds.

This was the backdrop for the creation of Burlington's Ethan Allen Engine Company No. 4 in 1857. It was one of four volunteer companies back then and was arguably the most prestigious, at least in terms of the number of prominent citizens on its rolls. Membership in the Ethans, as the company was called, was highly desired. As a social club, the Ethans had no equal. Their status was reaffirmed in 1888, when they opened the doors of their brand new firehouse building right on Church Street, one door from City Hall. But things were about to change.

Fire was a constant plague in the 1800s. The volunteer fire companies were great at parades and races and other pageantry. The club rooms were great retreats for Burlington's business elite to seek refuge from the pressures of daily life and to catch up on the latest goings-on around town. Many business connections and deals were no doubt made within their walls. But the one thing they weren't particularly good at was fighting fires. In their defense, firefighting infrastructure and equipment were primitive back then, and it's doubtful that professionals could have done much better. But as fire consumed more buildings, pressure began to build for the city to start to employ paid, full-time firefighters. At least they would be resident in the firehouses, meaning a much quicker response to fires. The members of the volunteer companies had to leave home, assemble at the firehouse and then head to the fire, resulting in a much slower response time. Burning buildings were often too far gone by the time they arrived at a fire.

So the city finally decided to replace the volunteer companies with a paid fire department in 1895. The volunteer companies were legislated out of existence. The Ethans wanted to maintain the bond they had formed, and the transition from fire company to social club for its one hundred active and honorary members was made. All of the other Burlington volunteer companies ceased to exist in any form. In 1897, the former Ethan Allen Engine Company No. 4 was formally chartered and renamed the Ethan Allen Club. Its nearly new firehouse on Church Street became fire station no. 1 for the new Burlington Fire Department, so the Ethan Allen Club had to find a new home.

An interior photo of the upstairs clubrooms of the firehouse of Ethan Allen Engine Company Number 4 on Church Street. *UVM Silver Special Collections.*

After having their quarters in rooms upstairs in the Walker Block on Church Street for a number of years, in 1905, the social club purchased the John Henry Peck house at 298 College Street. The 1834 mansion was one of the largest and finest homes in the city in its day.

The house had a very interesting history. John Henry Peck was a successful merchant in early Burlington. In 1853–54, the house was largely rebuilt in an outlay that amazed the people of the city. Mrs. Peck's boudoir alone cost $1,800 at a time when the wage of many laborers was under $1 a day. The other rooms in the house were finished on a lavish scale as well.

The rebuilt mansion was opened in August 1854 in the grandest housewarming ever known in Burlington. Guests from far and wide toured the home's conservatory, the first ever in the city, with great curiosity. The grounds were illuminated with locomotive headlights, and the Burlington Concert Band played. The equivalent of the Burlington area's "Four Hundred" showered the Pecks with congratulations and best wishes.

Two months later, John Peck's firm failed, with liabilities of over $1 million. Lawsuit followed lawsuit. The glory of the new mansion passed into legend. Mrs. Peck closed the blinds and doors, and they remained shut for the rest of her forty-four years. Not another guest crossed the threshold for the rest of her life, with the exception of a few funerals held at the home, including that of her husband, who died in 1874.

At her death in 1898, the home furnishings and Mrs. Peck's wardrobe and personal possessions were found to be much the same as they were on that festive night in 1854, reminiscent of Miss Havisham in Charles Dickens's *Great Expectations*. Now let us return to the Ethan Allen Club's tenancy of the Peck mansion.

Just after purchasing the Peck residence, the club built an addition to the structure that included a banquet hall, pool room and bowling alley. By then, membership had swollen to 250.

In the early twentieth century, there was an abundance of men's social clubs in Burlington. The Algonquin Club in particular seemed to mirror what the Ethan Allen Club had become—a club for the business and social elite of Burlington. If anything, the Algonquin Club was even more elite. There was talk of a merger, which ultimately didn't happen. The numbers favored the Ethan Allen Club; eventually, the Algonquin Club faded from the scene. There was later talk of merging with the Elks when the Ethan

The John H. Peck house, later the Ethan Allen Club, stood at 238 College Street. When the Pecks lived at the home a large glass conservatory existed on the west side of the house. It was the talk of Burlington at the time. *Author's collection.*

Allen Club was having a rough time financially, but its members voted to stay independent.

Along with its rooms and recreational facilities, the Ethan Allen Club boasted the finest restaurant in Burlington. It also offered the possibilities for what is now called networking. The club had no trouble attracting members; for many years, there was a waiting list to join. Membership was maintained at about five hundred.

Like all the old Burlington social clubs, the Ethan Allen Club was male only. But in 1931, it allowed a small concession to women, permitting wives of members to bowl at the club between 2:00 p.m. and 4:00 p.m.

In 1971, the 1834 clubhouse was destroyed—ironically, by fire. The following year, a modern clubhouse opened on the site of the previous club building. Membership continued strong through the '70s, with 515 members in 1982. And there was still a waiting list to join.

But by the mid-1980s, pressure had begun to build to admit women, which the club resisted. Women could enter the club only if accompanied by a member. The only entry open to unaccompanied women was a side door leading to the bowling lanes. It became awkward when Madeleine Kunin was elected governor and became the first governor not to get an honorary membership to the Ethan Allen Club. Several prominent members quit when the club refused to bend. The city tried to deny the club a liquor license due to discrimination.

But membership had started to slip, as membership in social clubs in general was declining. The refusal to admit women was hurting as well. In 1990, the club admitted its first woman member. But by then, the club was in a death spiral. By 2007, membership was down to 140, and that included 15 widows of deceased members, along with 5 female members.

The club closed in 2010. It was sold to Champlain College and, eventually, to the Greater Burlington YMCA, which demolished the 1972 club building and constructed a new YMCA building on the site.

10

HOTELS

Burlington lost five downtown hotels, four of which burned between 1906 and 1951. In the early days of the city, just about everything was downtown, including all hotels. The hotels discussed in this section include one located on Church Street, Burlington's main shopping thoroughfare, and four others located within a block of Church Street. Numerous other downtown hotels existed earlier than these five and are no longer around, but they stood so far back in time that no photos exist and history is scant.

THE AMERICAN HOUSE

The American House, later known as the American Hotel, was the oldest of the five lost hotels. The hotel building had its origins as the residence of a prosperous Burlington merchant named Jewett. In 1808, he built a large home on the southeast corner of Main and St. Paul Streets. It's unclear what happened to Jewett, but by the early 1820s, his mansion had been incorporated into a new Burlington hotel initially called Gould's Hotel.

Sources indicate that the hotel was built for a Montrealer named Parks and that in 1824 it was purchased by Vermont governor Cornelius Van Ness. He added a third floor and an east wing that extended well up Main Street. Van Ness leased the hotel to Royal Gould. Over the years, other owners of the hotel included Burlington notables such as Lawrence Barnes and Dr. B.J. Heineberg.

The American House, on the corner of Main and St. Paul, was the first real hotel in Burlington and, for many years, its finest. *Vermont Historical Society.*

In 1871, double verandas were added on the west side; a ladies' entrance was installed on that side as well. The same year saw the installation of the hotel's first steam radiators. The large cupola-style belvedere was part of the original 1808 Jewett house.

The hotel was elegant. The dining room was paneled in black walnut. The American was widely recognized as the finest hotel in Burlington for much of its existence. Presidents James Monroe, Martin Van Buren, Franklin Pierce and Ulysses Grant stayed at the American during their visits to the Queen City.

The verandas on the St. Paul Street side offered guests a look at the panorama of the lake and mountains to the west. Guests could take in this view, for which Burlington was justly famous, without leaving the hotel.

By 1883, the old American House had been acquired by the much newer Van Ness House across the street. Eventually, the American was open only during the warm weather months.

The American House was completely destroyed in a fire on December 16, 1906. A new venue, the Hotel Vermont, was built on the site of the American. Over time, it, too, came to be recognized as the best hotel in Burlington. Although it has not been a hotel for some time, the Hotel Vermont building still stands on the site of the old American House.

THE VAN NESS HOUSE

The Van Ness House opened in 1870 directly across St. Paul Street from the American House. It was named after former governor and American House owner C.P. Van Ness. In another connection to its rival across the street, the Van Ness was run by a longtime employee of the American House, O.B. Ferguson. Prominent citizens owned or managed the Van Ness over its long history, including former governor Urban A. Woodbury and Lemuel S. Drew, a wealthy stock breeder and developer of early Burlington. The Van Ness immediately supplanted the American as the best place to stay in town, and as mentioned earlier, the Van Ness ended up acquiring the rival American in 1883.

Like the American, the Van Ness was enlarged with later additions, particularly a large wing running down Main Street almost to the armory on the corner of Pine Street.

One immediate impact of the construction of the Van Ness was the blocking of the lake view from the American. The Van Ness exploited this advantage over the years, constructing an enclosed roof garden and then a "sunset promenade" walkway on the roof of a later addition running down Main Street.

On opening, the hotel advertised that a billiard hall, barbershop and bathrooms "are connected with the house." The hotel was diagonally across the street from City Hall Park and two blocks from the railroad depot. With a beautiful dining room highlighted by columns and support beams of ornately carved wood, the Van Ness quickly became the favorite for meetings, conventions and other gatherings.

The Van Ness emphasized safety in many of its advertisements. It featured an artesian well with a rooftop water tank to supply the needs of its guests. Burlington tap water was notoriously bad at this point in history,

The Van Ness Hotel is seen after it had been expanded several times, including the addition of the sun parlor on the roof and the large wing running down Main Street. A walkway called the Sunset Promenade allowed guests to enjoy the spectacular views from the hotel's roof. *Courtesy of UVM Silver Special Collections.*

with the water intake located close to the sewer discharge site in Burlington Bay. An 1895 ad for the hotel touted the water from its 360-foot-deep well. Another ad mentioned that the hotel featured a safety hydraulic passenger elevator, a fire escape and a Grinnell automatic sprinkler.

By the late 1800s, the Van Ness was the only Burlington hotel with verandas and the only building used exclusively for hotel purposes. Other hotels rented much of their ground-floor space to retailers.

On May 23, 1951, fire swept through the eighty-year-old Burlington landmark. The hotel was still doing excellent business—only 1 of its 137 rooms was not occupied at the time of the blaze. Late May is very pleasant in Burlington. The blaze did significant damage to the south wing, the older portion on St. Paul Street. The Main Street wing of the L-shaped hotel sustained far less damage.

The decision was made not to rebuild a hotel on the site. The contents of the hotel in the undamaged sections were put up for sale, and Burlington residents flocked to the Van Ness to scoop up bargains on furniture, linens, dishes and other items. Many of these purchases would end up in the summer camps of local residents. Many visitors were just looking for a piece of history.

When the building was emptied, the remaining structure was taken down. The debris from the hotel was trucked to a low area off Pine Street owned by Ray Unsworth, proprietor of the EB & AC Whiting Company. The remnants of the old hotel were dumped there as part of an attempt to raise the area, which was particularly prone to flooding.

The site of the Van Ness was sold to the Howard Bank, which built a new headquarters building there.

THE NEW SHERWOOD / MILNER HOTEL

The New Sherwood Hotel stood on the northwest corner of Church and Cherry Streets. A hotel had stood on that corner going back to the very early days of the city, well before the Civil War. The fifty-room Sherwood

The New Sherwood Hotel was the last in a line of hotels that stood on the corner of Church and Cherry Streets dating to before the Civil War. The seven-story hotel had large wings extending up Main and Cherry Streets. It became the Milner Hotel shortly before it burned in 1940. *Library of Congress.*

Hotel had been in business there since 1894. In 1911, a century-old wood-frame structure that was part of the Sherwood was demolished and a seven-story brick hotel was constructed in its place. It was immediately dubbed the New Sherwood.

Like the Van Ness, the New Sherwood was L-shaped. In addition to its Church Street frontage, the huge hotel sprawled well down Cherry Street. Its height enabled excellent lake views to be had from its roof, and a roof garden was soon added to take advantage of the view. The hotel was the tallest in the state of Vermont. Everything about it was big. The dining room sat 150 people, and the hotel featured a large exhibition hall.

As the biggest and newest hotel with all of the modern conveniences, the New Sherwood quickly surpassed the Van Ness as the favorite place for meetings and other gatherings. It was located on the city's main shopping street, and trolley cars passed by its front door.

The hotel featured ground-floor retail space, and one of these spaces was the location of one of the first real motion picture theaters in Burlington, when the World in Motion Theatre opened in 1911. It was the first theater in the city designed primarily for movies. The Royale Grill, a nightclub in the hotel, became a favorite spot for dining and dancing and featured bands from Montreal, Boston and other major cities.

For a time, one of Burlington's early dime stores, the long-forgotten A.A. Adams Company, occupied all of the ground-floor retail space in the New Sherwood. After a brief tenancy, the Adams chain went bankrupt. The New Sherwood space was then occupied by another national dime-store chain, the Grand Silver Stores. It, too, fell victim to the glut of dime-store chains and went bankrupt. The year 1927 marked the arrival of the first national chain on Church Street that was not a "five and ten cent store" when J.C. Penney announced its intention to locate a department store there. It occupied a small part of the New Sherwood space fronting Church Street. The hotel's second-floor dining room was reconfigured into the mezzanine of the new J.C. Penney store.

But in 1938, the hotel's large remaining ground-floor retail space was occupied by a national chain with a bit more staying power than the previous occupants. Sears, Roebuck and Company opened its first Burlington store there. Located just south of the J.C. Penney storefront, Sears' new Burlington store was much larger than its next-door neighbor. At nearly twenty-four thousand square feet, it was one of the largest retail locations ever in Burlington. It occupied the basement and two floors. Former hotel space given over to the new Sears store included the old grill location and dance floor, a kitchen and the hotel billiard parlor. Sears signed a fifteen-year lease with the hotel.

The year 1938 also brought about a name change, as the hotel was acquired by the national Milner hotel chain, and the New Sherwood became the Milner Hotel.

But less than two years after all these changes, the hotel was engulfed in flames in the early morning hours of February 14, 1940. The hotel was completely gutted, and the new Sears store was destroyed as well. The two hundred guests were all evacuated safely.

Although the hotel owners said they would quickly rebuild, the fire marked the end of the longtime presence of a hotel on the corner of Church and Cherry. The Milner chain did not rebuild. Sears, however, did, constructing a store on the old hotel site that was even larger than the one lost in the fire. It was Sears' third-largest store in New England at the time. The Sears and J.C. Penney Church Street stores both went on to serve as important parts of downtown Burlington's retail scene for decades. They eventually left Church Street for suburban shopping centers.

THE HOTEL BURLINGTON

Like the Van Ness and the American, the Hotel Burlington looked out on City Hall Park. Located on St. Paul Street across from the park, the location, like that of all the downtown hotels, was convenient to everything. But unlike the two other neighboring hotels, the Hotel Burlington never had a view of the lake and mountains to the west. It also didn't have a stand-alone building the way the other two did. Instead, it was located in one of several business blocks along that stretch of St. Paul Street. As a result, the Hotel Burlington was always seen as a notch below the Van Ness and probably on a par with the much older American.

Construction on the hotel started in January 1887. Less than four months later, the four-story brick hotel was completed. It's amazing how quickly large buildings were constructed in Burlington's early days. Like most large hotel and office blocks in town, the ground floor of the Hotel Burlington was given over to retail. The new hotel even succeeded in luring a tenant of the old American House to relocate to the Hotel Burlington.

The hotel did a steady if unspectacular business for years, always in the shadow of the Van Ness, commonly thought of as Burlington's best hotel at the time. Even though the Hotel Burlington was brand new, it could never command room rates as high as the Van Ness House.

So the Hotel Burlington was an affordable if unremarkable place to stay for most of its time. But it grabbed headlines on Saturday, January 8, 1910, when it was consumed in a fire that was whipped into a frenzy by a strong winter wind. Since the Hotel Burlington was not a stand-alone building, it shared a common wall with the neighboring buildings to the north and south. These walls were supposedly fireproof, but that did not prove to be

The Hotel Burlington was one of three downtown hotels that faced City Hall Park. All three eventually burned. *UVM Silver Special Collections.*

the case for the south wall. The fire broke through that wall and proceeded to destroy the entire adjacent Walker Block, a large brick business block that extended all the way to the corner of Main and St. Paul. The American House, located diagonally across the street from that corner, had burned to the ground in 1906, less than four years before. So the scourge of fire, which would do so much to transform the look of Burlington later in the century, got a good start around City Hall Park in the first decade of that century.

Another business block would rise in the place of the Walker Block, and it would contain another hotel, the Huntington, which followed in the footsteps of the Hotel Burlington as the low-cost option of downtown Burlington hotels.

THE WALKER LODGE

One final downtown Burlington hotel bears mention. When Willard Walker and former Vermont governor Urban A. Woodbury built the Walker Lodge in 1891, I think all would agree that it was a handsome building. It stood at 116 Main Street, directly across from the Van Ness House. The hotel was small, just two stories, built of brick with Georgian-style elements trimming it. It featured seven rooms on the first floor along with a large four-room owner's apartment. The second floor had thirteen rooms. The hotel had several long-term residents, including a music teacher and a clairvoyant who both held their sessions in their rooms at the Walker.

Willard Walker, like his father before him, was the manager of Burlington's Howard Opera House. He was also associated with the Crystal Confectionery Company, a large Burlington candy manufacturer. They had a store next to the Walker Lodge, at the corner of Main and St. Paul in the large Walker Block building, also owned by Willard's family.

All of this seems to have been too much for Willard. On August 4, 1898, his father was called to the sanitarium in Michigan where Willard was being treated because he was "not too well." He was transferred to a hospital in Battle Creek but died on August 13, 1898, at the age of thirty-four.

His widow, Lena, took over operation of the Walker Lodge. She lived there and ran the hotel for the next forty years. She bought out Governor Woodbury in 1903. In 1910, the entire Walker Block was destroyed in the previously mentioned fire that destroyed the Hotel Burlington. The fire severely damaged the Walker Lodge, but it was completely renovated

At twenty rooms, the Walker Lodge was by far the smallest of Burlington's downtown hotels. But its large rooms and the fact that the owner was in residence made it a favorite of long-term tenants. *UVM Silver Special Collections.*

and refitted shortly thereafter. Lena Walker finally sold the hotel in 1931. Photos from that era show the hotel still in like-new condition. But that would change.

The hotel changed hands a number of times and slowly descended into seediness. The neglected building deteriorated. It was the target of several arson attempts in the early '70s, and a few of its last years were spent as a homeless shelter. By 1982, the city had ruled the building to be unsafe, and the ninety-year-old structure was demolished on June 26 of that year.

11

THEATERS

With the advent of motion pictures, many storefront theaters opened in Burlington in the early part of the twentieth century. Most were just empty retail storefronts where rows of chairs were set up and silent movies projected on a wall, curtain or screen. Most were in business a very brief time, a few years at the most. All were located on Church Street or on one of its side streets. But once it became clear that movies were not a passing thing and that there was a potential to make a lot of money from them, more substantial, purpose-built theaters were erected in the city.

Burlington had two real movie palaces. The Strong (1904) was built originally as a venue for live performances and was later adapted into a movie theater. The Flynn (1930) was built just as vaudeville was in its final stages and was designed for movies while at the same time serving as an excellent location for live shows. The Flynn is still hosting live performances over ninety years after it opened; the Strong was lost in 1971.

THE STRONG THEATRE

The Strong has probably the most interesting history of all of Burlington's lost theaters. It was lost to fire, but if it hadn't been for an earlier fire, it may never have been built in the first place.

In the late 1800s, a group of Burlington businessmen built a large roller-skating rink on the current site of the Fletcher Free Library. It was built to take advantage of a roller-skating craze that had been sweeping the nation for several years. But not long after the Burlington rink was completed, the craze faded, and the rink became a bit of a white elephant. After serving as a furniture warehouse for several years, it became the armory for the local National Guard unit. But then the old rink had to be demolished or moved to make way for the new Fletcher Free Library.

Two brothers, J.J. and J.T. Whalen, bought the building with the intention of moving it. The seventy-two-by-two-hundred-foot wood building was cut in half and moved by horse teams one block down South Winooski Avenue to the corner with Main Street. There the building was placed on a foundation the brothers had built. The old armory was remodeled into an immense auditorium and dance hall, the largest in the state. But just as it was about to open, it was destroyed in a 1902 fire.

After considering their next move, the Whalens decided to go big. There was an increasing demand for a ground-floor theater in the city. The 1879 Howard Opera House was the city's only high-quality performance venue, and its third-floor auditorium was increasingly seen as a problem in the event of the need to evacuate in case of fire. The brothers engaged Frank L. Austin, a Burlington architect, to design a theater to rival or even surpass the Howard. He traveled to theaters all over New England, determined to incorporate the best ideas he saw into his new Burlington venue.

One of the challenges was the site, which was located in the deepest part of a ravine that snaked through the length of old Burlington. Rather than try to fill it in and risk building the new theater on filled land, Austin decided to build a foundation that stepped down the steep embankment into the ravine. This would prove to be a wise decision. In later years, some buildings erected on filled ravine land, including the Fletcher Free Library, faced problems due to settling.

The new Strong Theatre was huge. It sat 1,500 people and featured private boxes and two balconies, the only Burlington theater ever to be able to make that claim. The fifty-eight-foot-wide stage was capable of accommodating even the largest traveling companies. It was the most ornate theater ever built in Burlington, with molded plaster ornamentation on the ceiling, a proscenium arch, balcony fronts and opera boxes throughout the building. Painted scenes adorned the ceiling and proscenium. The stage was lighted by five hundred electric lamps.

The theater was the latest word in safety, too. It featured thirteen lighted exits, and even with a capacity crowd the entire building could be evacuated in three minutes.

When the Strong opened in 1904, it was widely praised on all counts. The city had never really seen anything like it. The Strong joined the Cahn and Grant theater chain, by far the biggest in New England, ensuring that the top acts touring the region would appear there. However, one major drawback to the design was the fact that many of the seats had views obstructed by columns. This was largely due to the presence of two balconies. The only sections that weren't behind columns were the front rows of the orchestra section (ground floor) and, ironically, the entire second balcony, which had the cheapest seats in the house.

Due to all the factors discussed here, the Strong supplanted the Howard Opera House as the city's top performance venue. In fact, the Howard ceased to operate as a performance house the same year the Strong opened.

As movies replaced live shows as the main entertainment in America, the Strong seamlessly switched from a vaudeville house to a movie house. A renovation in the '30s muted a lot of the interior's original ornamentation.

The 1904 Strong Theatre replaced the Howard Opera House as Burlington's premier performance venue. It segued smoothly into a movie house when motion pictures replaced vaudeville. It was one of the many buildings lost to arson fires in Burlington in the 1970s. *Courtesy of UVM Silver Special Collections.*

A new lighted Art Deco marquee was installed that extended well out over the Main Street entrance and highlighted the latest features amid an array of flashing lights.

But with the dawn of car culture, movie patrons came to prefer new cinemas in suburban locations with their acres of free parking. The old Burlington movie palaces, the Strong and the Flynn, one block away on Main Street, fell on hard times. The top balcony of the Strong was closed off, condemned as being unsafe. Both theaters became run-down and struggled to attract an audience.

But the Strong was a movie house to the end, which came on Saturday, October 9, 1971. *Klute*, starring Jane Fonda, was on the marquee when an early morning fire completely destroyed the sixty-seven-year-old landmark. The fire was determined to be arson, one of many such fires that plagued the city in the 1970s, claiming the Strong and other landmarks.

The fire left a literal gaping hole in the city's downtown, as the ravine location of the former Strong sat vacant for fifteen years. It was finally filled in 1987, when a new office building, Courthouse Plaza, was erected on the old theater site.

THE MAJESTIC THEATRE

The Majestic Theatre stood on the corner of Bank Street and South Winooski Avenue. Much smaller than the Strong, which was just down the street, the Majestic's initial seating capacity was only six hundred. Although it did have a stage for live shows, from the day it opened, May 16, 1912, the Majestic was primarily a movie house. It featured a four-piece orchestra that accompanied the silent movies featured in its early years.

It was built by J.R. Lockwood, a Burlington carriage maker, and E.R. Hutchinson, who had found success operating the Bijou Theatre out of a business block on College Street.

The much larger and ornate Strong was still primarily featuring live shows, so the Majestic was able to carve a niche for itself as a movie house. A year after the theater's opening, Lockwood and Hutchinson expanded the theater down South Winooski Avenue, knocking out a wall and increasing the length of the venue by forty feet. A new stage was put in the addition, while the old stage space was devoted to more seating, increasing capacity to seven hundred.

The American public was mad about the movies, and in the days before television and radio, people flocked to theaters. Features were changed often, sometimes daily, to create fresh demand and keep the crowds coming.

The Majestic can claim two distinctions in Burlington cinema history. It was the first theater built as a stand-alone movie house, and it was the theater where the first talkie shown in Burlington was screened, 1929's *The Wolf of Wall Street*.

Lockwood and Hutchinson sold the Majestic in 1923. It continued to do well for several more years. But by 1930, vaudeville was on its last legs. The Strong pivoted, becoming a movie house with only occasional live performances. The new Flynn Theatre opened in 1930, and it also focused primarily on movies from the day it sold its first ticket. Also in 1930, the new State Theatre on Bank Street opened. The State was a revitalized reincarnation of the Orpheum, which had been screening films at the Bank Street location since 1917.

So the Majestic was facing three rival theaters, all within a stone's throw of the venue and all more attractive in several ways than the aging Majestic.

The Majestic Theatre played third fiddle to the Strong and the Flynn for most of its existence. Seen here before the installation of its marquee in 1940, the Majestic was demolished in 1956 to make way for a gas station and parking lot. *Author's collection.*

The result was that the Majestic started to lose out with audiences. The newer, bigger theaters could outbid the Majestic for the top films. For many years, it was relegated to showing B movies.

The owners gave the theater a facelift in 1932, but the renovation didn't help much, as B movies remained the Majestic's stock in trade. A marquee was added in 1940. The Majestic was the last Burlington theater to get one.

The theater continued as a B movie house for the remainder of its life. But there was a market for B movies, and this enabled the Majestic to hang on until 1954. By that point, the pioneering theater was a distant fourth among Burlington's four venues. The doors were closed for good after the last showing of the film *Martin Luther* on Friday, November 5, 1954. In keeping with its long history of showing second-tier films, not one recognizable name appeared in that movie. After it closed, the Majestic sat vacant for over a year. The building was eventually demolished in February 1956. A gas station replaced the venerable movie house. A gas station / convenience store and parking lot still occupy the large footprint of the former theater.

THE STATE

The 1930 State Theatre would never be confused with a movie palace. It was small, occupying space in the old Walker Block on Bank Street. It didn't have a large, ornate lobby, just a small area between the ticket booth and the theater doors where the concession stand was located.

The ancestry of the State went back to the early days of cinema in Burlington, to the 1911 World in Motion Theater located in the New Sherwood Hotel. In 1917, the proprietors of the World in Motion, Catherine and Meader Martin, bought the old Walker Block, previously the Burlington Grocery building, from Alfred Perrotta. Perrotta had started the Orpheum Theater in his building just a few months earlier. The Martins ran the Orpheum until 1930, when they renovated it and renamed it the State Theatre.

Meader Martin died in 1937, but his wife, Catherine, continued to operate the State until 1951. At this point, Ernest Handy started renting the theater while Catherine retained ownership of the building, which by now included the Black Cat Café next door. The Black Cat was a popular Burlington restaurant and nightclub.

When Catherine Martin died, she left the Walker building and the theater to the Roman Catholic Diocese of Burlington. The diocese quickly sold it

The State Theatre on Bank Street is seen in 1967. The marquee shows that the feature playing that day was *The Graduate*, starring Dustin Hoffman. Despite having a much smaller seating capacity than the Flynn and the Strong, the State was always able to attract top movies to its screen. *Courtesy of UVM Silver Special Collections.*

to Handy, who had been renting the State for seven years by this point. He would run it until it reached the end of the line.

Despite its small size relative to the rival Flynn and Strong theaters, the State was always able to hold its own in attracting top movies to its screen. A good example of this is the fact that the Vermont premier of the film version of *The Sound of Music* was held there. This wildly popular movie with strong Vermont connections was no doubt highly sought after, but somehow the State managed to get it. Maria von Trapp herself attended the opening. The State also hosted the Vermont premiers of *2001: A Space Odyssey* and *The Graduate*, which coincidentally is the movie shown on the State's marquee in the photo featured in this book.

But toward the end, the State, like other downtown theaters, was struggling in the face of competition from suburban cinemas. By the mid-1970s, the theater had been reduced to featuring X-rated fare in an attempt to attract customers. The end for the State came on May 1, 1977, when an explosion in the building started a fire that was soon out of control. The entire Walker Block building, including the State and the neighboring Black Cat Café, was destroyed. The fire left Burlington with only one remaining movie theater, the Flynn. Before long, that struggling venue would get out of the movie business, undergo a complete renovation and transform itself into Burlington's premier live performance venue.

The location of the State would later be the site of Burlington's first McDonald's. The Golden Arches did not receive a warm welcome from Burlington residents, and the king of fast food was gone within a few years. Another restaurant, not a national chain, stands there as this is written.

12

RECTORIES

F or many decades, members of the clergy were some of the most important figures in the life of Burlington, especially the leaders of churches and parishes. The members of a congregation wanted the dwelling of their leader to reflect how much they valued him and how important he was as a member of the Burlington community. Consequently, a pastor—and a bishop even more so—would normally be housed in a grand home, even a mansion. These were nearly always located close by, often next door to the church. Whether they were called rectories, parsonages, vicarages or other names, these were buildings for which no expense was spared.

CATHEDRAL RECTORY

The huge building that was the rectory of the Cathedral of the Immaculate Conception was located on Cherry Street, right next to the cathedral. It was initially designed to be the residence of the Roman Catholic bishop of Burlington. Its first resident was Bishop Louis DeGoesbriand, one of the most revered members of the Catholic clergy in the history of the city and of the state of Vermont. He was also a prolific builder, erecting churches and other buildings in Burlington and all over Vermont. Even well after his death, he inspired the building of the Catholic hospital in Burlington that bore his name.

Built as the home for Bishop Louis DeGoesbriand, this building spent most of its life as the rectory for Cathedral Parish. Bishop DeGoesbriand was temporarily buried in the front lawn of the rectory until the crypt underneath the cathedral was finished. The rectory was lost in the 1972 fire that destroyed the Cathedral Church. *Courtesy of the Archives of the Burlington Catholic Diocese.*

The immense residence for the bishop was completed in 1885. It was a three-story, stone and brick building erected in the French Second Empire style, with a mansard roof typical of that design. A four-story tower on the west front broke up the otherwise symmetrical look of the building. Large porches on the east side of the building led to a covered passageway connecting to the church. The edifice cost $20,000, a huge sum in 1885.

It's a bit disingenuous to keep referring to it as the bishop's residence. He did live there, but so did the cathedral pastor and curates (assistant priests), and in the early days, there was also a boarding school in the building. So, in addition to being the bishop's residence, it was also the cathedral rectory.

Bishop DeGoesbriand came from a very wealthy noble family in Brittany, France. But he lived a very simple life, channeling his personal wealth into the various building projects and church-related charities that he was operating. It is not recorded what he thought about the rather magnificent residence that his parishioners constructed for him.

When Bishop DeGoesbriand died in 1899, he was buried in a temporary grave in the front lawn of his residence. After lying there for three years, in 1902, his body was moved to a crypt that had been recently completed under a mortuary chapel on the east side of the Cathedral Church.

The bishop of Burlington continued to reside in the Cherry Street rectory until 1910. At that point, the church's national policy was to start moving bishops from rectories into private residences. A large home on the corner of Maple and South Prospect was purchased, and Bishop Joseph Rice moved out of the cathedral rectory and into the newly purchased home.

The Cherry Street rectory continued on as the residence of the cathedral pastor and curates. At the high-water mark, there were five curates plus the pastor assigned to the cathedral, so there was still ample room in the rectory.

The building would have been a Burlington landmark had it stood off by itself somewhere else in the city. But rectories are destined to always be in the shadow of their churches. And so it was with the cathedral rectory. It shared the fate of the Cathedral Church when the church burned in 1972. Flames from the burning church spread to the adjacent rectory. After the fire was extinguished, both the cathedral and the rectory were burned-out shells.

THE "BISHOP'S HOUSE"

After moving out of the cathedral rectory, the bishop of Burlington resided for a time at a home on the corner of South Prospect and Maple. Then, in 1918, the diocese purchased one of the largest old homes in the city, a twenty-six-room mansion at 52 South Williams Street. The house, which had eleven fireplaces, stood on a large parcel of land typical of the old estates in the Hill Section of town. A semicircular driveway enabled carriages to pull up to the house and return to the street without turning around, another feature often found at Gilded Age estates in Burlington.

The house had a lot of history. The original house was built in 1854. In 1886, the estate was purchased by Albert E. Richardson, one of the founders of Burlington's Wells Richardson patent-medicine company. He was one of the wealthiest men in Burlington, and he doubled the size of the house. Among his many changes was the addition of a large circular tower to the front of the building. The interior was finished off in spectacular fashion, featuring stained glass and light oak wood trim of all sorts throughout the house.

After the turn of the century, Richardson suffered a series of financial reverses and lost the house. It was taken by his creditors and was vacant for

The former home of wealthy businessman A.E. Richardson became the residence of Burlington's Catholic bishop and the chancery office in 1918. Its sale to the Medical Center Hospital of Vermont, which proposed tearing it down for a parking lot, sparked a protracted battle with those trying to save the building. Although that battle was lost, it marked a turning point. Historic properties in Burlington would no longer be torn down without a peep of opposition. *Courtesy of UVM Silver Special Collections.*

three years until the diocese purchased it in 1918. In addition to housing the bishop, 52 South Williams also served as the chancery office for the diocese.

By the 1970s, Burlington had a new bishop, John Marshall, installed in early 1972. A mere six weeks after his installation ceremony, Burlington's Cathedral Church was destroyed by fire. In March 1977, it was announced that the 125-year-old bishop's house and grounds had been sold to the Medical Center Hospital of Vermont. Marshall broke with the long tradition of bishops (Catholic and Episcopal) living in splendid mansions and moved into an apartment in the old St. Joseph's Orphanage building on North Avenue.

The hospital announced its intention to tear down the old mansion and replace it with a 177-car parking lot. By this time, historic preservation had gained a lot of traction. No longer could a Burlington landmark be knocked down without a peep of opposition, as had happened so often in the past.

The reaction to the announcement of the hospital's plan was swift and loud. The mayor and many prominent lawmakers announced their opposition to the proposed demolition. Letters to the editor added the voices of citizens to the chorus of opposition. A grassroots group called Save the Bishop's House was formed. Prominent attorneys worked for free to try to find a legal angle to delay or stop the razing of the mansion.

But all of these efforts could only postpone the inevitable, as there was no legal way to stop the hospital from carrying out its plan. After a battle to save the residence that lasted two years, the historic property fell to the wreckers on June 2, 1979.

A small silver lining in this dark cloud was the fact that the interior woodwork, chandeliers and several fireplaces were removed and preserved before the house was taken down. Some of the woodwork was installed in the historic Grasse Mount building, owned by UVM, so it's now in safe hands. But most of it was sold by the antiques dealer who purchased it from the hospital. The dealer then sold it to a party who had it installed in the former Mill restaurant and bar in Winooski. The restaurant was in a former millworker housing building that was being converted into an upscale restaurant called the Mill Café and Boarding House. That venture did not last long, but the next restaurant, the Peking Duck House, had a long run in that space, where for many years diners marveled at the spectacular decor surrounding them as they enjoyed their meals.

But an irreplaceable landmark was lost for probably the worst outcome imaginable: a parking lot. That lot is still there today. The hospital did construct a tall brick wall on South Williams Street to obscure its parking lot from view. I will leave it to the reader to analyze that.

ST. PAUL'S RECTORY

The rectory for St. Paul's Cathedral was yet another gift from John Purple Howard. He left Burlington at a young age and made a fortune in the hotel business in New York City. He never returned to Burlington except for an occasional visit, spending his retirement years traveling the world. But his love for his native city remained strong, as evidenced by the numerous generous gifts he made for major building projects in the city.

He was an Episcopalian and a lifelong supporter of St. Paul's Cathedral in Burlington, which would have been there during his early years in the city. The cathedral's chapel was one of his many gifts to the church.

In 1883, Howard made an offer to the parishioners. He would donate a new rectory to replace the old one, built in the 1830s. It had served as the

The 1885 rectory survived the fire that destroyed St. Paul's Cathedral and chapel but was ultimately lost as part of a land swap between the parish and the developers of Burlington's urban renewal project. *Courtesy of Tom Little.*

home of the church's rector since 1850. All agreed that the rectory was "not in keeping" with the other splendid church buildings around it.

Howard often attached conditions, always easily attained, to his gifts. In the case of the St. Paul's rectory, one condition was that the parishioners raise $2,000 to furnish the building, an amount that was quickly obtained.

Another, somewhat odd condition, was that he be given the old rectory building. Why he would want the building is a mystery. The answer was known only to Howard.

The new rectory was completed in the spring of 1885. It stood on the northeast corner of Pine and Banks Streets. The building was a modified Queen Anne style with fourteen rooms. It was three stories tall, with the third story being a large, steeply roofed attic. The ground floor was constructed of light red stone from Willard's quarry, while the second floor was of wood and shingled. The front entrance featured a stone archway supported by columns, constructed of Isle LaMotte gray stone. Two massive, ornate chimneys flanked the building. A large porch on the west side of the residence completed the package.

The St. Paul's rectory would be the last in the long list of John Purple Howard's gifts to Burlington. He died in England about six months after the rectory was completed. His world travels ended, his body was returned to Burlington and is buried at Lakeview Cemetery.

After serving as the residence of the pastor of St. Paul's for nearly a century, the rectory was lost as an indirect result of the fire that destroyed the cathedral in 1971. This is detailed earlier in this volume, but to recap, although the cathedral and chapel were destroyed, the rectory was undamaged. But the loss of the church buildings resulted in the land they stood on being involved in a land swap with the developers of the new

Burlington Square Mall. The parishioners of St. Paul's agreed to swap their lot for a much larger parcel on the corner of Pearl and Battery, where they built their new cathedral. The undamaged rectory thus came into the possession of the developers, who tore it down along with the fire-damaged church buildings in April 1972.

13

GOVERNMENT BUILDINGS

THE 1830 COURTHOUSE BUILDING

When the city of Burlington was in its early days, a plot of land was set aside to serve as Burlington's version of the town green seen in many New England towns. Traditionally, one or more churches, the town hall, the courthouse and probably the general store could be found facing the green in most town configurations.

In Burlington, it happened a bit differently. Perhaps befitting the city's emphasis on industry, tourism and commerce, what ended up around the town green for the most part were stores, hotels and banks. But on the east side of the green, one of the first buildings was a courthouse. The area quickly came to be called Court House Square, now City Hall Park.

Burlington's first courts were held in 1790 in Gideon King's tavern on King Street, a building that still stands. In 1797, Burlington's first real courthouse was constructed in the middle of the town square. That courthouse was replaced four years later by a larger one.

That second Burlington courthouse was lost to fire on June 16, 1829. A replacement was erected in 1830. The new structure, Burlington's third courthouse, was a brick Federal-style building. It was two and a half stories, with the stone basement level rising well above the ground. The structure had two chimneys built into the walls on each gable end, typical of the Federal style. A large cupola topped the building. It had steps leading to entrances on the Church Street as well as the Court House Square sides of

The 1830 courthouse was Burlington's third. After the more familiar 1871 courthouse opened on lower Church Street, this building became the first location of the Fletcher Free Library. *Vermont Historical Society.*

the building. Town offices were in the basement, and courtrooms were on the third floor. For much of the latter part of the nineteenth century, a fire company was housed in the basement.

This courthouse served the community well, but as the town grew, it became inadequate. A new courthouse was constructed on lower Church Street in 1871, rendering the old facility redundant. It was swiftly put to new use, however. Mary Fletcher and her mother had gifted the city with a $10,000 bequest for the purpose of starting a city library. The money was to buy books, and the only condition attached to the funds was that the city provide a space for the library. The old courthouse, being available and conveniently located, was the natural choice, and so it became the home of the new Fletcher Free Library.

Burlington's library remained there until 1904, when the Andrew Carnegie–funded Fletcher Free Library building opened on College Street. The old courthouse was vacated again. During its last years, it housed the Stannard Memorial Hall. George Stannard was a prominent Civil War general from the area. The memorial hall served as a Grand Army of the Republic (GAR) hall and then as a hall honoring veterans of later wars. The building was used for all manner of public events.

As the building was approaching the century mark, it was demolished in late 1925 to make way for a new Burlington City Hall.

OLD BURLINGTON CITY HALL

This building stood just south of the old courthouse discussed earlier. It was built in 1854, and its front entrance was on the west side of the building facing Court House Square. Unlike the old courthouse, it did not have an entrance on the Church Street side. A fairly basic square structure, its dominant features were a gabled front entrance flanked by large columns and featuring a balcony on the second floor. Probably the building's most memorable feature was its large central dome.

Unlike the courthouse, the City Hall building did not have an entrance on the Church Street side. The main entrance fronted on the circular park that developed on Court House Square. As Church Street became more important in the commercial life of Burlington, the building increasingly seemed to be facing the wrong way. While pedestrians and cars thronged Church Street, the main entrance to City Hall looked out on a bucolic park with dirt lanes for buggies. Eventually, the lane was eliminated, the park squared off and the lawn extended right up to City Hall. A city street never passed by the front entrance of the old building.

Like the courthouse, this building was two and a half stories, with a stone foundation. The rest of the building was brick. In the early days, it served as police headquarters in addition to housing city offices. A small portion of the building was rented to retail establishments. As with the old courthouse, a fire company was also housed in the basement of City Hall.

The building included a performance space, a scarce thing in the city until the Howard Opera House opened in 1879. Many plays, dances and other

Burlington's old City Hall dated to the 1850s. It was a true multipurpose structure, housing a performance space, a firehouse, retail and even a roller-skating rink in addition to government offices. It was torn down to make way for the current City Hall building. *Vermont Historical Society*.

events were held there. For a time during the roller-skating craze in the late 1880s, the City Hall building hosted roller-skating during the winter.

The building served Burlington well for many years and was still solid when the city decided that it had to come down. The old courthouse and the old City Hall had served the city well as multipurpose buildings for years. But by the late 1920s, the growing city realized that it needed a new, larger City Hall building so that it could consolidate most city departments under one roof. At the same time, the city would build a new central fire station and a new performance/exhibition building (Memorial Auditorium). So, in late 1925 and early 1926, the old City Hall building was taken down to make room for the new City Hall. The new municipal building would be built on the land formerly occupied by the old courthouse and the old City Hall.

The loss of this landmark was mitigated by the fact that its replacement, designed by the McKim, Mead and White of New York City, is a splendid building in its own right. The firm corrected the lack of an entrance on Church Street. The new building features identical entrance doors on the park and Church Street sides. A wide set of stone steps leads to the ceremonial first-floor entrance on the park side. On the Church Street side, two sets of stairs lead up to the second-floor entrance.

THE OLD CUSTOM HOUSE / POST OFFICE

Former Burlington architect Ammi Young had been appointed the supervising architect of the U.S. Treasury Department. His 1859 Custom House and Post Office building stood for many years on the southeast corner of Main and Church Streets. Although Young is listed as the architect, it's likely that much of the work on this design was done by his staff.

The building was a very simple affair, a basic cube with arched windows on the ground floor and rectangular ones on the second floor. A low railing

Burlington's 1859 Post Office and Custom House is pictured after the mansard roof was added ten years after it opened. It was replaced by the monumental marble Federal building that still stands on the corner of Church and Main Streets. *Vermont Historical Society.*

and four projecting chimneys topped off this minimally ornamented structure. In 1869, a third floor was added featuring a mansard roof. This greatly enhanced the look of the building while adding needed space. The post office was entered via triple arched doors on the Church Street side, while the customhouse was accessed through a single arched doorway on Main Street. This reflected the much heavier volume of traffic generated by the post office.

For decades, the U.S. Customs Service was one of the most important agencies in the nation. Until the imposition of the income tax in 1913, customs duties were the primary source of income for the government. The agency enjoyed a favored status in Washington. The post office was an important part of people's everyday lives, bringing letters, packages and other communications. For many years, it was people's only link to the outside world.

The importance of these two agencies was reflected by the decision to build a new, much larger post office and customhouse on the site of Ammi Young's 1859 building. The old building was leveled in 1902 and replaced by the monumental marble building that still stands on that spot today.

THE CHITTENDEN COUNTY COURT HOUSE

Built in 1871 of red stone from the nearby Willard's quarry on Shelburne Road, the old Chittenden County Court House was a lovely French Second Empire building. The lines of its mansard roof were broken in front by a tower on the north side of the building topped with a crown of iron filigree. For over a century, that tower was a common sight in photographs of the Burlington skyline. It's a bit of a stretch to say that the city had a skyline. Tall buildings were nearly nonexistent; the skyline consisted mainly of steeples and towers like this one. Nonetheless, the courthouse was one of Burlington's signature buildings.

But as the building aged, it was neglected. The building had been allowed to deteriorate for many years. A leaking roof caused timbers to rot, resulting in structural damage. Finally, after years of neglect, it was reported on January 10, 1982, that money to repair the building would be in the proposed Chittenden County budget for the following year. A month later, a fire raced through the building, badly damaging the courthouse.

But the exterior walls remained in place, and much of the magnificent woodwork was undamaged. The fire debris was removed, but a bitter battle

The 1871 courthouse was a true Burlington landmark, its tower gracing the city's skyline for over a century. Its demise was a result of a complicated mix of neglect, fire and a desire for a new courthouse by Chittenden County judges. *Vermont Historical Society.*

was about to begin over the fate of the remaining structure. By this time, the city had lost enough historic buildings that a preservationist movement had taken shape. Called the Burlington Civic Trust, the group fought for months to save the courthouse from the wrecking crew. The position of the Chittenden County assistant judges, who were the decision makers in the matter, was that the building was unsafe and must be torn down. They had been casting about for a new courthouse building for a number of years.

The Civic Trust engaged an architecture firm from Boston to assess the building. Its report said that the remaining structure was sound and that it could be restored for about the same price that demolition and new construction would entail. Armed with this, the trust waged both legal and public relations battles to fight demolition. Picketing, impassioned letters to the editor and other PR tactics called attention to the cause, while trust lawyers were able to obtain court orders to delay the razing of the structure. Coverage in the *Burlington Free Press* was extensive.

In late June, demolition of the remaining structure began. Outraged preservationists said that this was in violation of a court order they had obtained delaying demolition. They rushed to the scene to try to stop the destruction of the building. Burlington Health and Safety inspector Steve Goodkind had issued a permit for portions of the building that posed a safety hazard, such as the tower and chimneys, to be taken down, but not the whole building. When he saw what was happening, he tried to serve a stop work order on the contractor but was prevented from doing so by Chittenden County sheriff's deputies.

Contrary to the county's assertions that the walls were on the verge of collapsing, the stone walls proved to be difficult to bring down. At the end of first day of demolition, the front wall was still standing.

On August 9, the Vermont Supreme Court decided that the county was within its rights to take down the building. By then, the courthouse had been gone for six weeks.

In December 1982, the interior woodwork that had been salvaged was sold at auction. The array on offer was impressive: a black walnut grand staircase, a mission oak staircase, one thousand linear feet of two-inch-thick chestnut door and window casing, twenty-five Victorian doors and on and on. As it was being auctioned, one expert present said that it would cost at least $100,000 to reproduce the woodwork today, if it could be done at all. The whole lot ended up being bought by Montreal millionaire developer Marvin Gameroff for $2,000. He was flabbergasted at the price, declaring that he had been prepared to go as high as $20,000 if the bidding took him there. Gameroff committed to keep the woodwork in Vermont, to be incorporated into an expansion of the 1833 Green Mountain Inn in Stowe, which he owned.

Notices appeared in the paper offering bricks and stone from the old courthouse for sale, and after that it disappeared into history.

OLD CHITTENDEN COUNTY JAIL

In the very early days of the city, Burlington's jail was located on the top block of Church Street. But as that street became the center for shopping and just about every other type of business in town, it became apparent that a better site for the jail was needed. So, in 1888, a new Chittenden County jail was constructed on the northeast corner of Main Street and South Winooski Avenue.

The new jail was called a model facility. It featured a round cage that the jailer rotated by turning a crank. Prisoners were delivered to the various cells on each floor by means of this rotating cage. This minimized the chance of an assault on the guard and discouraged escape attempts by sawing through bars, as prisoners were regularly rotated to different cells.

As was the style at that time, the jail building included a large living area for the jailer and his family. The jailer's dwelling was a large two-story brick structure with a mansard-roofed, third-floor attic. The cells were located in a large octagonal wing attached to the north side of the jailer's residence. The jail was designed to hold thirty inmates.

The Chittenden County Jail is seen in 1906. The jailer's residence is at the left, while the octagonal section at the right housed the prisoners. It featured a unique rotating central cage for delivering prisoners to cells, which minimized the chance for an assault on a guard. *Author's collection.*

This jail served the county well for decades, but by the 1970s, it was obsolete. It was too small, the building was worn out and the site lacked outside space for exercise and other activities. The 1888 jail was finally replaced by the new Chittenden County Correctional Facility in South Burlington. The old building was torn down in 1975, and the site is now a parking lot.

14

CHURCH STREET BUILDINGS

Church Street has been Burlington's main shopping street going back to the early days of the city. Initially, College Street was where merchants located their stores, but when the Central Block opened on the corner of Bank and Church in the early 1860s, that started to shift. In fairly short order, homes on Church Street started being converted into stores or leveled and replaced by more business blocks.

Church Street is located a few blocks from the waterfront, the source of the city's wealth for well over a century starting with the opening of the Champlain Canal in 1823. Burlington became a transport and manufacturing center, and the wealth generated found its way into the pockets of the many merchants who set up shop on the street to cater to the needs and wants of the growing city.

In early photos of Church Street, it has an almost ramshackle, Wild West appearance. Many of the older homes that were converted to stores had wood awnings installed across their fronts. These somewhat slapdash-looking establishments were complemented by numerous Federal-style brick buildings up and down the street and an ever-growing number of large brick business blocks.

The street continued to evolve over time. Horse cars ran up the street from 1885 to 1893 and were then followed by an electric street railway, which ran trolleys on the street until 1929. As the automobile started to dominate, the street was paved and became a two-way street for cars. Eventually, cars were banished, and the street became a pedestrian marketplace.

Lippa Jewelers storefront of black glass, stainless steel and mirrors was typical of the sleek, modern look that many old stores adopted in the 1930s and '40s, transforming the look of Burlington's Church Street shopping district. *Courtesy of UVM Silver Special Collections.*

The wood awnings were replaced with canvas retractable awnings. Overhead signs were hung out over the sidewalk by the majority of merchants. Most signs were illuminated at night. But by the 1930s, the street had a distinctly unmodern look to it. Many storefronts dated to the 1800s, and the street needed a facelift. That process began in 1931, when Abraham's Drug Store gave its old storefront a modern makeover. The street level was done over in Carrara black glass and stainless steel, giving the store a sleek, modern look in the Art Deco style. The upper floors were clad in enameled steel panels, again in the Art Deco vein. Dozens of stores would follow over the years, modernizing the rather tired-looking stores on Church Street and on several side streets as well.

The 1960s saw another drastic change, as nearly every overhead sign on the street was removed. This purge was subsidized by a local developer who owned several properties on the street and wanted to remove the signs to give the street a modern look. Many of the old overhead signs were worn and needed repair. Only two overhead signs from the old days survive on Church Street. Ironically, one of them is now considered a Church Street icon. The Optical Center clock (formerly the Bero Jewelers clock), next door to the old Abraham's store, has been hanging over the street for more than a century, and it would be unthinkable to try to remove it now.

The top of the street has three landmark buildings that anchor the street, the 1816 Unitarian Church at the top of the street gave the street its name and is a classic New England church, providing a unique focal point for the city's downtown. Just across Pearl Street stands the 1897 Masonic Temple and the 1895 Richardson. Both are huge, classic structures.

The street continues to evolve. There is only one old Federal-style building left, Abraham's building, but the Federal elements are now hidden behind the Art Deco cladding. The sleek black glass and stainless storefronts are all gone.

Most of what has been torn down on Church Street over the years has been done in an organic progression as new buildings replaced old, outdated structures. All of the wood-frame former residences are gone. A few brick business blocks were taken down, most notably the pre-1900 Barrows Block, which formerly housed F.W. Woolworth, and the 1930 S.S. Kresge building. The former was replaced by a modern Woolworth building, and the latter was removed to provide an entrance to the new Burlington Square Mall from Church Street.

But Church Street has suffered several disastrous fires that destroyed two large landmarks, the 1889 YMCA building and the New Sherwood / Milner Hotel. The Milner is discussed in the hotels chapter of this book. Fire also visited the top block of Church Street on several occasions, taking out some smaller buildings each time. A large fire in 1929 destroyed another large business block, also named the Barrows Block, across the street from Woolworth. But by far the biggest fire in the history of the street was the 1974 Centers fire. The largest of these fires is covered separately.

THE OLD YMCA BUILDING

Constructed in 1889 on the southwest corner of College and Church Streets, the YMCA building was a joint project between the YMCA and Samuel Huntington, who for many years had maintained a stationery store / bookshop on that corner. The YMCA was an important civic organization in Burlington, and the substantial headquarters that it put up reflected that.

The large stone and brick building housed retail establishments on the street level, as was the case with every large building on the street, be it the opera house, a hotel or a business block. The large gymnasium of the YMCA and meeting rooms were on the upper floors, as were numerous offices available for rent. The entrance to the YMCA on the College

The old YMCA building at Church and College Streets dominated that corner for forty years. After it burned in 1928, the YMCA departed for South Union Street, and a much smaller building replaced it. Stone elements of the old entrance were incorporated into the new building, and scorch marks from the 1928 fire can still be plainly seen. *Courtesy of Emily Speiser.*

Street side of the building and the entrance to Huntington's store on the building's corner both featured beautifully carved brownstone elements with terra-cotta trim.

The huge building was a prestigious address. Businessmen like John J. Flynn, one of the most important men in Burlington's history, had offices there. On the ground floor, important tenants included the Wright Clothing store and Bailey's Music Rooms.

If you were in the YMCA building, there was no need to list an address in your ads or even mention the corner of Church and College. All that needed to be said was that you were in the YMCA building. Everyone knew where it was.

But on February 1, 1928, the handsome structure went up in flames. The immense building was a total loss. The interior was gutted, and several exterior brick walls collapsed onto the street. The YMCA relocated to a new building on the corner of College and South Union Streets. The Wright Clothing store merged with the F.D. Abernethy department store and relocated to the Richardson at the top of Church Street, becoming part of the new firm of Abernethy, Clarkson and Wright. Bailey's Music Rooms relocated a little farther up College Street. McAuliffe's Stationers, successors to Samuel Huntington, built a handsome but much smaller brownstone structure on the corner of College and Church. The corner entrance is very similar to the old Huntington entrance, and in fact it incorporated elements such as the columns from the old entrance into the entrance to the new building. Charring from the 1928 fire can still be seen on those columns. The names *Huntington* and *McAuliffe* are carved in stone above the entry to the new stationery store. Because the new entrance is so similar to the old one, many confuse the McAuliffe's building with the long-gone YMCA building.

F.W. WOOLWORTH / BARROWS BLOCK WEST SIDE

The national five-and-ten-cent store chain of the F.W. Woolworth Company opened a store on Church Street in Burlington in 1899 on the corner of Church and Cherry Streets. The storefront featured Woolworth's trademark "red front" with gold letters spelling out the company name.

By 1937, Woolworth needed additional space, so it took out a fifteen-year lease on the building to the south of its existing location. The company did

The old F.W. Woolworth store is seen being demolished in 1964. The "Kathleen Tower" can still be seen standing atop the remaining portion. The bell tower of St. Paul's Cathedral is visible in the background. *Courtesy of UVM Silver Special Collections.*

not immediately occupy the entire newly leased building. The Fashion Shop continued there until 1943.

That building leased by Woolworth, known as the Barrows Block, was unique in that it featured a tall tower on top of the business block. Known as the Kathleen Tower, it was erected by Augustus and Mary Barrows when they built the Barrows Block in 1893. The tower was built to memorialize their daughter, Kathleen, their only child, who died at the age of three in 1886. Between the two large arched windows on the front of the building they had a terra-cotta plaque installed with just the word *Kathleen* on it surrounded by decorative filigree. The building came to be known as the Kathleen Temple, or Temple Kathleen, a usage that faded after Mr. and Mrs. Barrows passed from the scene and the reason for the tower was largely forgotten.

Mr. Barrows never got over the loss of his daughter. He died at fifty-three in 1897. His wife outlived him by thirty-two years, but she continued to memorialize Kathleen until her own death by using rents from the Barrows Block to fund the education of young girls in the community.

Well after the Barrowses were both gone, their memorial tower continued to loom above Church Street. It was there from the day the Barrows Block opened in 1893 until it was demolished in 1964. The tower can be seen in many postcards and photos of old Church Street. It has caused a lot of head-scratching over the years.

S.S. KRESGE / JUPITER

In 1926, Woolworth's great rival in the dime-store business, S.S. Kresge, opened a large store next to the Barrows Block. Kresge was supremely confident that its Burlington store would be a success. The company took out a fifty-year lease on a large store that stretched from 47 to 55 Church Street. It also took out an option for another forty-nine years after the fifty-year lease expired. Interestingly, Kresge's landlord was the Home for Aged Women (later known as the Converse Home). The Kresge parcel was one of three large downtown properties owned by local charities. The others were the Howard Opera House, which John P. Howard had gifted to the Home for Destitute Children in 1888, and the Bank Street lot that Henry's Diner sat on. It was jointly owned by Henry Couture of Henry's Diner and the Home for Aged Women.

Kresge's storefront was nearly a carbon copy of Woolworth's. It featured the same red front above the store's front doors, with the name *S.S. Kresge Co.* in gold letters across the red background. The Kresge name was bracketed on either side by the letter *K* and the phrase *5 and 10*, also in gold.

Detroit-based Kresge followed New York–based Woolworth in many other respects. Both stores featured long soda fountains and hardwood floors, and both were packed with low-cost merchandise that made them a shopper's dream. Even kids could find something they could afford at these stores. People still reminisce about the creaky floors in both establishments.

In May 1938, the still relatively new Kresge store suffered a disastrous fire, destroying everything to the outer walls. The company hired local contractor Wright and Morrissey to rebuild the store, a feat that was accomplished in an amazingly short span of six weeks. The new store opened on July 28, 1938. It featured the largest soda fountain in Vermont, sixty-eight feet long, with thirty-one seats upholstered in red leather.

The 1930 storefront of the S.S. Kresge five-and-ten-cent store was a near carbon copy of the F.W. Woolworth's "red front" with gold letters. On Burlington's Church Street, the two dime-store chains stood right next to each other. *Courtesy of UVM Silver Special Collections.*

In 1943, Woolworth finally occupied the rest of the Barrows Block when the Fashion Shop moved out. This meant that the two dime-store giants became neighbors, sharing a common wall. They would remain so until the end of their runs in Burlington. Neither left for the suburbs, probably due to their leases as much as from any sense of loyalty to Church Street.

The two buildings occupied by Woolworth, which were much older than Kresge's, were torn down in November 1964. A modern Woolworth store opened on the site a year later. The new store did business for another thirty-three years, finally closing in late 1998. Woolworth was on Church Street for a century, and even though it was a national chain, the store is as fondly remembered as just about any store that ever did business downtown.

Not long after Woolworth tore down its old storefronts, in 1965, Kresge gave its 1930s store an update. Gone was the venerable "5 and 10" identifier. Kresge emerged from the makeover as Jupiter, one of two discount rebrandings that replaced the Kresge name. The other, chiefly used in large stores in shopping centers, was Kmart.

Jupiter was in business on Church Street for less than a decade. Mondev, one of Burlington's urban renewal developers, had acquired the building, and in 1974, it was demolished to provide an entrance from Church Street to Mondev's new Burlington Square Mall.

BARROWS BLOCK EAST SIDE

There were two Barrows Blocks on Church Street. The one on the west side was the home of F.W. Woolworth from 1899 until 1964, when the block was torn down. The Barrows Block on the east side was the home of the Boston Store, a very large and important department store in early Burlington. The Barrows Block that it occupied was four stories tall and spanned from 52 to 58 Church Street.

The entire Barrows Block was destroyed in a 1929 fire. It's been gone so long that no one alive remembers the Barrows Block or the Boston Store. The Boston Store had actually gone out of business by the time of the fire, but numerous businesses that had moved into its old space on the first two floors of the block were lost in what was one of the biggest fires in Burlington's history. This was a major fire that changed the look of that block between Bank and Cherry Streets significantly. The scene of the fire sat vacant for a while, and it so happened that during this period the United States was undergoing a mania for miniature golf. Burlington followed the fad, and mini-golf courses sprang up all over the area, both indoors and outside. The former site of the Boston Store became an outdoor miniature golf course for one summer. Miniature golf was a passing fancy that soon ended, but downtown retail was a real and steady thing. Soon, two new buildings rose on the lot vacated by the fire. Both were to be occupied by national chains. Montgomery Ward filled the north part of the space and W.T. Grant the south part. Montgomery Ward did business on Church Street until it moved to much smaller quarters on College Street in 1961. W.T. Grant moved to the Shelburne Road Shopping Plaza in 1962.

M.H. FISHMAN / CENTERS

The M.H. Fishman Company was unique, because even though it was a regional chain, it was based in Vermont. The company was started in 1917 in Rutland by Meyer Fishman. Eventually, he grew the company until it had over fifty stores from Maine to Alabama. Fishman's was what you would call a "dime store," but rather than the typical sign indicating it as a five-and-ten-cent store, Fishman's storefront signs read "M.H. Fishman 5¢ to $1.00 Stores." A bit more honest perhaps.

There were numerous Fishman stores in Vermont, including in Rutland, of course, as well as St. Albans, St. Johnsbury and Vergennes, to name a few. But the largest Vermont Fishman's outlet was in Burlington. That store opened on Church Street in 1929 in the middle of the block between Bank and Cherry Streets. The first storefront was fairly small, but business was good enough that Fishman's dramatically expanded its store in 1948.

In its 1948 expansion, Fishman's increased its footprint more than fivefold. It was now bigger than neighboring Grant's and Ward's, both of which had previously dwarfed Fishman's. The newly expanded store also featured a sizable basement area as part of the store. To enable the expansion, Fishman's had to feature a new L-shaped footprint. This resulted in its having a second entrance on Bank Street. The Bank Street storefront was actually much wider than the old entrance on Church Street. The new store featured a huge soda fountain / lunch counter, one of the biggest in Burlington, along the east wall of the store.

The 1920s storefront, which was looking dated by the late '40s, was replaced by an ultramodern, somewhat monolithic-looking storefront. It extended up all three floors of the building and had rows of glass blocks

The Church Street façade of the Centers discount department store. The L-shaped store also had a prominent storefront on Bank Street. It was one of the largest stores ever in downtown Burlington. *UVM Silver Special Collections.*

instead of windows. It was probably the most modern storefront ever on a building in downtown Burlington.

As the 1950s progressed, suburban shopping centers began to eat into the business monopoly that old downtown centers had enjoyed for so many years. Another trend was the rise of discount stores. These were usually huge and offered discounted merchandise in a no-frills, self-service mode. Several discounters had already sprung up in the Burlington area, including Gaynes, Forest Hills Factory Outlet and Grand Way. In response to this trend, Fishman's opened its own series of discount stores under the name of Centers. The Burlington store was rebranded as a Centers, and coincidentally, its longtime next-door neighbor on Church Street, W.T. Grant, left downtown for the suburbs in 1961. Centers expanded into the old Grant space, creating a massive store, one of the biggest ever in downtown Burlington.

But on July 19, 1974, Centers was completely destroyed in yet another of the series of fires that plagued the city in the 1970s. The Centers fire is often described as the biggest blaze in the history of the downtown area. There were several pre-1900 fires on the industrial waterfront that were probably bigger.

In addition to the giant L-shaped Centers store, a half-dozen small retailers and a new branch bank located south of Centers' Church Street storefront were also lost. These structures were in the oldest wood-frame building remaining on Church Street. Also destroyed was the huge brick building housing the Lash Furniture business, located just east of Centers' Bank Street entrance. The fire was truly massive.

The large two-story building to the east of the Lash building, housing Empire Launderers and Cleaners and James Hair Styling, was not significantly damaged by the fire. However, city officials saw the damage as an opportunity to build a large parking garage in this area. The undamaged building ended up being torn down to make way for what became known as the Cherry Street parking garage.

The portion of the destroyed area housing the smaller retailers was filled by a new brick business block. Centers officials talked about rebuilding, but that did not happen. The portion of its footprint that was formerly W.T. Grant became a small storefront on Church Street. The rest of the old Grant space became an alleyway leading to the new parking garage from Church Street. The rest of the devastated area, along with several nice old Victorians on South Winooski Avenue, became the site of the previously mentioned parking garage.

15

UNIVERSITY OF VERMONT BUILDINGS

Burlington is lucky in so many respects to be the home of the University of Vermont. Among the benefits the city enjoys due to the school's presence is the wealth of beautiful buildings that the university has on its campuses. Mainly concentrated on the central campus green, the array of spectacular university buildings has no doubt played a role over the years in convincing many students that UVM is the place for them.

The city is fortunate that the university not only built these architectural gems but also has the wherewithal to maintain them properly, a very expensive proposition. The stewardship of the college had also resulted in an enviable record of avoiding the loss of buildings to fire. This is in marked contrast to the many great buildings that have burned over time in Burlington, as has been outlined in previous chapters of this volume.

In its very early days, UVM did suffer the loss by fire of its original main building in 1824. But since then, the list of university buildings that have come and gone is largely made up of structures that were torn down intentionally and were not particularly beautiful or architecturally significant. Buildings such as the three "shoebox" dorms (Chittenden, Buckham and Wills), the Carrigan dairy building, Commons Hall (the Hash House), the Cook Physical Science building and others fall into this category. Two large historic mansions were torn down to make way for the Waterman Building, but their replacement was a more than worthy successor. But there were a few university buildings whose loss merits discussion here.

ANGELL HOUSE

Angell House was constructed in 1869 under the supervision of UVM president James Angell as a home for the college's presidents. It was a French Second Empire, two-story brick building with a third-floor attic with a mansard roof. A large one-floor wing extended to the north. The house was prominently located on the University Green, as were all of the school's buildings in those days. President Angell lived there, followed by presidents Matthew Buckham and Guy Benton. By 1917, Angell House had become Angell Hall and was used as a women's dormitory.

But in 1925, prominent UVM benefactor James Wilbur donated money for the construction of a chapel to be known as Ira Allen Chapel. The chapel was to be one of the most impressive buildings on campus, designed by the most prestigious architecture firm in America, McKim, Mead & White. The brick building would feature a 170-foot-tall bell tower.

Given the prominence of this new building and the extreme generosity of Wilbur to UVM in the past, it was agreed that it should be built on University Row, joining other landmark donated buildings such as the Billings Library and the Williams Science Hall. But there was no room left on University

Angell House served as the residence of UVM presidents and as a women's dormitory before being torn down to make room for the Ira Allen Chapel. *Author's collection.*

Row for another building, and the obvious choice for removal was Angell Hall. Thirty years earlier, faced with a similar situation, UVM had moved Torrey Hall to make way for Williams Science Hall. Angell Hall was similar to Torrey Hall in size and weight, but the college opted to demolish it rather than try to move it. So in the spring of 1925, Angell Hall was torn down.

OLD UVM MEDICAL COLLEGE BUILDING

The Old UVM Medical College Building was donated in 1884 by one of Burlington's greatest benefactors, John Purple Howard. In 1883, Howard purchased the old Levi Underwood mansion at the "head" of Pearl Street. The large residence was completely remodeled inside for its new role as a medical college building. The building replaced the outdated medical building located in the current Pomeroy Hall on the south end of the UVM Green. Howard's new building was located on the northern end of the green, at the intersection of North Prospect Street and Colchester Avenue.

The handsome building was of brick, with three stories, the third of which was described as a "French roof" (mansard). The mansard roof featured two circular dormer windows on all four sides. The roof was topped by a large central cupola/belvedere with walls of glass on all sides to make available the spectacular view from this tall building that stood near the top of Burlington's Hill. The front and side entrances featured porches with fluted columns. Above the front entrance was a projecting gable with the words *Gift of John P. Howard* carved in stone and set into the arch above the gable. Just below that, another stone with the words *Medical College* sat above the second-floor window.

A large extension off the back was also topped by a mansard roof.

Inside the building, a large marble slab was carved with words thanking Howard for his gift. Its last line was the Latin quote *Si monumentum requiris circumspice* ("If you seek his monument, look around you"). The quote was first used in Christopher Wren's St. Paul's Cathedral in London.

The new building was state of the art for its time, equipped with a large lab with forty available microscopes and a huge amphitheater seating 368 persons. The roof of the amphitheater was thirty-four feet high, nearly as high as the auditorium of the Howard Opera House. The spacious new medical building came at a very opportune time, as UVM's medical school had graduated a record class of 101 the year before.

The second medical college building at UVM is seen here. It was a renovated former residence, and John P. Howard paid to have the old mansion transformed into a state-of-the-art teaching facility for the School of Medicine. Destroyed by a fire caused by careless smoking in 1903. *University of Vermont Silver Special Collections.*

But this tremendous building would have a very short life on campus. Less than twenty years after it opened, it was destroyed in a fire on Wednesday, December 2, 1903. Students noticed smoke coming from the floorboards in the amphitheater. The fire was later determined to have been caused by a lit cigar that was discarded and fell between the floorboards.

Despite the fact that the lost building was underinsured, the university was able to quickly construct a replacement building on the site. The much larger 1905 medical college building, which still stands, served in that capacity until 1970, when it became John Dewey Hall, the location of the UVM psychology department.

UNIVERSITY FARM

With the passage of the Land Grant College Act in 1862, the University of Vermont became a land grant college. The act, sponsored by Vermont congressman Justin Morrill, granted 30,000 acres of land for each member of Congress to every state (except those in open rebellion against the Union). Vermont had three congressmen and two senators when the act was passed, so it got 150,000 acres to sell. The states were to use the funds raised from selling the land to establish colleges. UVM was the only New England state university that was already in existence when the act was passed.

Morrill's act stipulated that land grant colleges should teach the "practical arts," chiefly engineering and agriculture. This was a dramatic departure from the classical education provided by most colleges and universities up to that the time.

UVM used the proceeds from the land to establish a College of Agriculture, which quickly merged with the university proper, becoming the University of Vermont and State Agricultural College in 1865.

One important feature of the university resulting from all of this was the establishment of the UVM Farm on Williston Road, just east of the main campus. On the north side of the road, a complex of farm buildings grew up over time, with barns, silos, sheds, animal pens and a large farmhouse

The UVM farm in the 1940s. The buildings sat on the north side of Williston Road, while cultivated fields were on the other side. For many years, the first thing travelers saw as they approached Burlington from the east were the cows and chickens of the farm. *Author's collection.*

residence for workers. Beyond the buildings to the east stretched a large area of fenced-in pastureland on which the school's dairy herd grazed. Scattered about on this land were numerous henhouses, and chickens wandered about freely.

Across the street from this, on the south side of Williston Road, stretched acres of open fields used to raise crops. This area was part of the school's Agricultural Experimental Station, where all kinds of new techniques and new plant species would be tried out in a continuing effort to improve crop yields, insect resistance and so forth. Although the city of Burlington was largely industrial at this point, in the rest of the state, agriculture was by far the dominant business.

Since Williston Road becomes Main Street as you enter Burlington, the farm sat on the main entrance road to Burlington from the east. Generations of travelers and locals became used to seeing cows grazing and hens pecking, along with barns, silos and other indicators of farm life as they entered the Queen City.

But as the university and the adjacent Mary Fletcher Hospital grew, by the 1960s, the land that the farm sat on had become needed for additional building and parking by both institutions. So, in 1965, a new UVM farm was constructed on Spear Street in South Burlington. This also became a familiar sight, as it was easily visible from both lanes of the new Interstate 89. Meanwhile, the old farm buildings were torn down, and the fencing was removed from the pasture. The site of the former UVM farm is now largely occupied by parking lots and buildings for UVM and the University of Vermont Medical Center, the successor to Mary Fletcher.

16

THE LOST NEIGHBORHOOD / URBAN RENEWAL

Not all losses are of historic or irreplaceable buildings. In the 1950s and '60s, the nationwide urban renewal program hit home in Burlington. This well-meaning program provided federal money to incentivize cities big and small to eliminate blighted sections of town and replace the structures that had been removed with modern development, both commercial and residential. It all sounds positive, but the way urban renewal played out in the Queen City was a disaster for the families who lived in the zones designated for removal and redevelopment and, in many respects, for the city as a whole. Although this happened over fifty years ago, for many who were directly affected, the wounds are still fresh.

The urban renewal area comprised a total of twenty-seven acres. It covered six entire city blocks, part of another and the entire west side of Battery Street that bordered the three-block-long urban renewal area. The zone contained 124 buildings, all but 2 of which were privately owned. All 124 were slated for destruction. The neighborhood was the location of Burlington's "Little Italy," where the city's Italian immigrants had put down roots, opened Italian grocery stores and restaurants and developed a cohesive, close-knit community between the city's waterfront and its downtown core.

Once it had been decided that this was the area to be cleared, residents not only had to live with the threat of losing their homes, but they also had to read and listen to repeated reporting referring to their neighborhoods as blighted and even as slums. The federal money that was to flow to Burlington was considerable, and it was in the city's interest to portray the

Merola's Market at 35 Cherry Street was an institution for several generations in the neighborhood known as Burlington's "Little Italy." It was one of numerous businesses ended by having the misfortune of being located in the zone cleared for urban renewal. *Courtesy of UVM Silver Special Collections.*

area to be removed in as negative a light as possible, as the entire point of urban renewal was to remove substandard, old housing. The first step in this process was a citywide vote in April 1958 in which the voters were asked to admit that the city had slums. This admission was the first step toward getting federal funding. Burlington's mayor at the time, in a bit of hyperbole, said that the worst slum areas in Vermont were along Battery Street in Burlington and that they were "at least as bad as anything in the United States." He was not alone. Many felt the need to make the blocks chosen for clearing appear as bad as possible. The voters agreed that the city had slums.

There is no doubt that some structures in the removal zone were in bad shape. But to portray that entire area as blighted was grossly misleading. The area contained numerous buildings that were significant architecturally, historically or both. The two buildings not in private hands were the Converse School and the Sara Holbrook Center. Converse is discussed in an earlier chapter. It was almost certainly the most magnificent school building ever erected in Burlington. Sara Holbrook, on lower College Street, was in a gorgeous twenty-room Victorian mansion from the 1800s.

The blocks on lower College included numerous other grand homes, and large historic Victorians were scattered throughout the twenty-seven acres. Numerous pre–Civil War structures were in the area to be cleared. Across Pine Street from Converse stood the old Mathews mansion, a large brick building that was the site of the Ready Funeral Home when urban renewal first came calling. Just down Pine Street from the Converse School stood the old Doolittle-Crane house, a large historic brick home dating to the 1840s. The zone included Burlington's oldest existing school building. The area also included numerous businesses, including Bernardini's Italian Restaurant; several markets, including longtime neighborhood mainstay Merola's Italian Market; two longtime city bakeries, Girard's and Mother Moquin's; and several others. While many of the other homes may not have been Victorian showplaces, they were not rickety firetraps, either. They were simply good, solid houses that had provided a home for generations of Burlington families. Maybe some needed a paint job or other TLC, but to say they all were slums needing to be bulldozed was overkill of the worst kind.

Compounding the matter was the fact that the urban renewal plan would cut off numerous through streets. St. Paul, Pine, South Champlain, Bank and Cherry Streets would all have sections cut off by the plan, disrupting

Burlington's 1893 Converse Grammar School, its tower gone, awaits the wreckers in 1966. It was probably the most prominent of a number of historic buildings taken down as part of Burlington's urban renewal effort. *UVM Silver Special Collections.*

a smooth-flowing grid that had worked well since the city's earliest days. Those streets are still blocked off today.

The 1972 fire that destroyed St. Paul's Cathedral resulted in that entire block being included in the urban renewal zone as a result of a land swap. Initially, just the northern half of that block was to be leveled, but with the loss of the cathedral, the southern half ended up in the hands of the urban renewal developers. As discussed earlier, the 1885 St. Paul's rectory, a large historic stone building undamaged in the fire, was added to the list of buildings to be torn down.

Needless to say, all of this caused no end of controversy. Loud voices for and against the urban renewal plan made their opinions known in letters to the editor, in articles, at public meetings and so forth. Historic preservation was still on wobbly legs at this time, and one doesn't see it cited in contemporary reporting as a reason to oppose the urban renewal plan. The main issue cited by those against the plan was the loss of the neighborhood, whose residents became active and impassioned opponents of the plan to dislodge them.

But the residents were far from alone. Many notable public figures came out in opposition. The most vocal was Belmont Frank, a longtime North Street retailer then living in Florida. Frank took out many huge ads in the *Burlington Free Press* outlining his case against urban renewal from every possible angle. It was a bad deal for the city, it would hurt downtown, blocking off streets would cause traffic nightmares, among other arguments. He sometimes went a bit overboard and was dismissed as a crank by the pro–urban renewal forces. But many other, arguably more credible voices formed a mounting chorus of opposition to the plan.

The debate raged on for years. But the city and the developers promised numerous benefits. The displaced families would be fairly compensated for their properties and placed in better housing. The city would benefit from the modern hotels, stores, apartment and office buildings and parking garages that would be constructed in the cleared area. The prospect of a modern civic center to replace the 1920s Memorial Auditorium was dangled. The waterfront would be revitalized, bringing economic benefits to the city and its people.

The process moved forward in fits and starts, and in May 1964, the city started purchasing the first properties within the urban renewal zone. This ignited an entirely new round of controversy, and many homeowners objected to what they saw as woefully inadequate offers being made by the city for their homes. Many of the homeowners appealed their cases, and a city official whose job it was to defend the city's offers in the appeals process confided later that he was embarrassed to have to try to justify the offers the city was making. Some offers were adjusted upward, but it's safe to say that when one factored in the value of the properties, along with the disruption of people's lives by being forced out of longtime family homes, loss of neighbors and ending up living somewhere people really didn't want to be, no city offer came close to making up for what happened.

In May 1966, the first demolitions were carried out. There were still 150 people living in the zone to be cleared at this point. Most of the buildings were cleared in 1966–67, but it took over four years until the last building in the area was demolished, in October 1970.

The aftermath didn't really make anyone feel better about the loss of their homes. Much of the cleared area remained vacant for many years after demolition. The structures put up in place of the lost neighborhood were modern, charmless boxes. The Cherry Street parking garage and the Burlington Square Mall, centerpieces of the urban renewal development and downtown Burlington's supposed answer to suburban malls, were both demolished in the late 2010s.

The mention of urban renewal even today, well over fifty years later, still generates a visceral reaction from many who were impacted.

17

MISCELLANEOUS

BATTERY PARK'S FOUR CANNON AND RAMPART

During the War of 1812, Burlington's Battery Park was the site of an earthen rampart and a battery of cannon that were installed to defend the city from an expected attack by British troops in Canada. Thousands of American troops were garrisoned in and around the park area. But other than a British ship that fired a few cannonballs harmlessly at the slope below the park, the attack never materialized.

But the name stuck, and this part of Burlington was set aside perpetually for parkland, not so much because of its history but rather because of the sweeping views of the lake and mountains to the west to be had from the western edge of the park. The park sits well above the lake just below and offers an unobstructed view that makes the park a mandatory stop for any tourist visiting Burlington.

The old cannon from the War of 1812 went elsewhere when the war ended, but in 1895, Congress granted four Civil War–era naval cannon to Burlington as part of a national dispersal of Civil War–era artillery. The city arrayed the four cannon on huge slabs of stone in a row along the very western edge of Battery Park, recreating at least some sense of the historic battery of cannon that once stood there. In addition to the cannon, the city received one hundred cannonballs. These were stacked in pyramids on stone platforms flanking the park entrance. Others were stacked near the cannon.

The four cannon that once lined the western edge of Battery Park are seen along with remnants of the 1812 earthen rampart in this 1900 photo. *Courtesy of Emily Speiser.*

Vestiges of the old 1812 rampart could still be seen for decades after. Even after 1900, one could still see a raised portion of the park that followed its western edge. But by the 1930s, a wide walkway was cut into that edge of the park, and a modern road for autos was then laid beside the walkway, substantially raising the level of the land on that side and eliminating the last indication that there was once a rampart there.

After the rampart was no more, the replacement cannon soon followed. In October 1942, the Burlington Board of Aldermen voted to contribute all four cannon and the one hundred cannonballs to the scrap drive in support of the war effort. They would add seventeen tons of metal to be melted down for armaments. At the last minute, it was decided to keep one of the cannon, and only nineteen of the one hundred cannonballs could be found.

That solitary cannon still stares out over the lake and has been a favorite photo spot for locals and tourists ever since it's been there. As far as the missing eighty-one cannonballs, city officials admitted at the time that they had no idea what happened to them. No doubt many of them reside in homes in the area to this day.

THE BURLINGTON RAVINE

The first settlers of Burlington encountered a very unusual topological feature in their new village. A long ravine snaked through the middle of the town, stretching from what is now Riverside Avenue to the north, to lower Church Street, opposite the Converse Home at its southern end.

The early settlers basically ignored the ravine at first. There was plenty of available land to build homes and businesses on, so the city grew up on both sides of the ravine. As roads were built connecting Burlington to neighboring towns, bridges were constructed over the ravine at what would become Pearl Street, Main Street and Shelburne Road.

With the coming of the Rutland Railroad in 1849, the Vermont Central quickly built a spur to Burlington from its Essex Junction depot to compete with its rival for the lucrative business being generated from Burlington. To reach Burlington's waterfront, the Vermont Central routed its tracks through Burlington using the ravine. This eliminated the usual problems involved with running a railroad through an existing city. The wooden bridges that had been built over the ravine became railroad overpasses constructed using large stone blocks.

Author Henry James visited Burlington in 1870, and he mentions the ravine in his account of his visit. He tells of taking a stroll from his hotel up the hill to the university. "I followed a long street which leaves the hotel, crosses a rough, shallow ravine, which seems to divide it from the ugly poorness of the commercial quarter, and ascends a stately, shaded residential avenue to no less a pinnacle of dignity than the University of Vermont."

Once the Vermont Central's tunnel under North Avenue was completed in 1861, that became its new route to the waterfront, and the tracks in the ravine were abandoned. This created a new role for the ravine, as an unofficial sewer and trash dump for the city. Since the city had neither a sewer nor a dump for many years, citizens had to find their own way to dispose of trash, garbage and sewage. For many, the nearest steep slope was the most convenient way to get rid of all types of refuse. The slopes of Riverside Avenue and the city's Intervale floodplain became common dumping grounds for those living near them. But because the ravine undulated through so much of the city, for many citizens, this was the nearest place to do their dumping. For many years, trash and garbage of all sorts accumulated in the ravine. When the city ran its first street sewers, the pipes terminated in the ravine. From there, everything eventually washed into Lake Champlain.

The deepest part of the Burlington ravine cane be seen sloping down steeply from the back of the 1871 Chittenden County Courthouse in this 1878 photo. The flat area at the bottom of the slope was once a large pond. *Courtesy of UVM Special Collections.*

Eventually, the city did build a sewer line in the ravine. This separated the sewage from everything else going into the ravine, but the sewage still ended up in the lake. The ravine became a common dumping point for the many wagonloads of sawdust and wood shavings generated daily by the city's waterfront mills and factories. So, slowly, the shallower parts of the ravine started to fill up. Homes were built on it, and neighborhoods formerly divided by the gulch were united.

But the deeper parts of the ravine, particularly at the northern end and the area east of the intersection of Main Street and South Winooski Avenue, continued to be used as illegal private dumps well into the twentieth century. The stench from the rotting refuse of previous generations made summer near certain parts of the ravine unbearable. This was often accompanied by hordes of flies. Punctuating this were regular fires that broke out in the ravine due to spontaneous combustion, which often proved exceedingly difficult to extinguish, as the fire was deep below the surface.

Since the intersection of Main and South Winooski was at a main entrance to the downtown area of the city, the presence of trash fires there was an embarrassment, as were the hundreds of large rats that prowled around it. A private dump, called Hyland's Dump, had been run there for years. It was the biggest dump in the city, in a very deep section of the ravine, and a fire was almost always smoldering in it. One reporter said that the smoke rising from Hyland's pit gave the impression of a volcano at the corner of Main and South Winooski.

Eventually, this dump was closed, but the sections of the ravine around this area would prove to be unstable due to the settling over the years of improper fill. The Masons wanted to build their huge new Masonic Temple on the corner of College and South Winooski Avenue, but their engineer told them that there was no way that the filled land there would support the massive structure. The much smaller Fletcher Free Library did end up getting built on that corner and was nearly lost due to structural damage caused by settling.

In most of Burlington, the old ravine is imperceptible, but remnants of it remain. The deepest part of the ravine never did get filled in. The best place to still see the ravine is King Street between South Winooski Avenue and Church Street. The old Strong Theatre lot to the north and the old Hood Plant to the south both have structures whose builders decided to build down into the ravine rather than try to fill it at its deepest point.

THE ELMS

Burlington was certainly not unique in once having many of its streets lined with American elm trees. Just about every city on the Eastern Seaboard planted elms on its streets in the 1800s. The American elm was seen as the perfect street tree for cities. It was hardy. Even the winters of northern cities like Burlington were no problem. It was fast-growing, rising three to six feet a year in its early years. It lived a long time. Out in the country, an elm could live to be six hundred years old. The life of urban trees is much shorter, but it can still reasonably be expected that elms planted in a city can live to be three hundred years old. But the main attraction of elm trees for urban planners was the fact that they formed their stately canopy high above the street. And because of their great height, their branches would form archways over the streets. This provided a shady canopy, cooling the streets in the heat of the

Mature elm trees form an archway heading down College Street in this 1900 image. Sigma Phi fraternity house is seen at the right. *Library of Congress.*

summer and creating unforgettable street views. Elms were pretty much universally viewed as the perfect city tree.

In the very early days of Burlington, Lombardy poplars were planted along the city's then unpaved streets. An infestation of worms killed those trees off. They were replaced by yellow locust trees, which featured luxuriant foliage and attractive blossoms. The prevalence of locust trees is evidenced by the fact that Elmwood Avenue was previously named Locust Street, after the trees planted on the sides of that street. But borers killed off most of the locust trees. Next to be tried were native sycamores, but they succumbed to a blight.

So Burlington joined hundreds of other cities in planting elms, and nothing but elms, along its streets. Burlington's elms were planted periodically throughout the middle of the 1800s. By the middle of the 1900s, the city's elms had matured. The result was what one writer described as "a city in ambush, almost concealed in a forest." Looking down major streets like College, Main and Shelburne, the elms arching overhead created a streetscape that was never to be forgotten by anyone who saw it.

At its high-water mark, around 1960, Burlington had around ten thousand elm trees. In addition to lining many streets, they also graced city parks and were particularly prominent in Battery Park, City Hall Park and on the University of Vermont Green.

Despite the fact that Burlington's elms were over a century old, its citizens fully expected that many more generations would be able to enjoy them due to their long life expectancy. But it was not to be, as nature had other ideas. Like the poplars, locusts and sycamores that preceded them, Burlington's elms fell victim to a natural pestilence in the form of Dutch elm disease. It first appeared in Burlington in 1957 and soon began to work its way through the streets and parks of the city. Virtually every street tree in the city was an elm, and nearly 100 percent of them were killed by Dutch elm disease. The 1960s witnessed the sad spectacle of the city's elms being cut down. Burlington went from being a "city in ambush" to a naked city in just a few short years. When the trees were gone, the contrast could not have been more

The shade from the elms in Burlington parks provided a cool refuge from the heat of the city's summers. Citizens line the benches in City Hall Park in this photo from around 1900. *Library of Congress.*

stark. The city has not looked the same since. The streets looked barren with the elms gone. The variety of replacement trees that have been planted over the years guarantee that the city will never again lose all of its street trees at once. But the new trees simply lack the majesty of the American elm.

Burlington's elm-lined streets now exist only in memory and photographs. But those who were around when the elms were creating their cathedral-like arches, their "crowning glory," over the city's streets will never forget them.

THE CITY OF SOUTH BURLINGTON

It may seem a bit unusual to include a neighboring city in a book like this. But the creation of the town of South Burlington in 1865 constituted a monumental loss for the city of Burlington. One veteran observer of the local scene who has deep knowledge of the city's history termed Burlington's agreement to create the town of South Burlington by far the greatest mistake ever made by the city.

As the town of Burlington was originally constituted, it had an area of about forty-five square miles. But the growth of the town was centered in the area around the waterfront. The vast majority of the forty-five square miles was farmland, with isolated farmhouses and farmers' fields occupying most of the acreage to the east and south of the waterfront area and downtown.

The waterfront area of the town of Burlington was industrial and a transportation hub. The university was there. It was a city of mills and factories, and with each passing year, the differences between the urban majority and the rural minority became more pronounced.

The farm dwellers did not see why they should have to help pay for sewer improvements to alleviate the notoriously bad city water, which was resulting in outbreaks of typhoid among residents. The farmers got their water from wells or streams, and it was fine. Conversely, Burlington officials balked at having to maintain the many miles of farm roads that connected the farms in the rural areas of town.

So, in 1864, a new Burlington City Charter was drawn up. Section 1 of the charter laid out the boundaries of what would be the new city of Burlington. Section 29 of that charter stipulated that all land outside of the boundaries described in Section 1 would become the new town of South Burlington. This charter was approved by the state legislature in 1865.

The net effect of this was that Burlington gave up nearly thirty of its forty-five square miles of land to create South Burlington. The grant included miles of exquisite shoreline, with some of the most beautiful lake and mountain views in the country, and some excellent beaches. The agricultural land that made up most of the new town was prime farmland, mostly flat, with rich soil and located in the Champlain Valley, which has a milder climate than most of the rest of Vermont due to the presence of the lake. This was some of the best farm country in the state.

What South Burlington did not get was people. In the first census, conducted five years after the creation of the town, South Burlington had a mere 791 residents, while Burlington had 13,596. No doubt the Burlington city fathers figured that they still had plenty of room to grow in their fifteen square miles, and they had retained what they felt was important, including many miles of waterfront extending north from the city center to the mouth of the Winooski River.

But they did not take the long view. Now, over 150 years later, the city of Burlington has developed to the point where available land for building new housing developments is nearly nonexistent. Recent new housing units have been created mostly in high-rise buildings. The city has to build up, since it can't build out any more. Large housing developments are being constructed in surrounding towns such as Williston and, of course, South Burlington, as much of the former farmland is going into housing. Burlington International Airport sits in South Burlington, because Burlington did not have a large parcel of flat land capable of accommodating the airport.

As the town of South Burlington evolved from a farming community to a prosperous suburb of Burlington, it has seen tremendous growth over the last half century. It is now the second-largest city in Vermont, trailing only its old parent, Burlington.

In 1865, Burlington did retain one small section of its former territory within the new town of South Burlington. That was the Burlington Poor Farm, located just south of the new Burlington city limits. South Burlington was paid $851.53 for the sixty-acre poor farm property, which included significant lake frontage. Thirty-seven years later, Burlington would sell the property for $9,200. Those sixty acres are worth millions today.

THE SLIDES AT ETHAN ALLEN PARK

Since Ethan Allen Park opened around the turn of the nineteenth century, it has been generally considered to be the jewel of the Burlington public parks. In addition to hiking trails, picnic areas and a playground, the park also featured spectacular views from the forty-foot Ethan Allen Tower and a lookout called the Pinnacle. The park proved so popular that in 1905 the Burlington Traction Company began work to extend its trolley line from its terminus at Institute Road to the park three-quarters of a mile beyond.

In the late 1920s, the Burlington Park Department installed the largest playground slide in America at Ethan Allen Park. The Everwear Manufacturing Company's thirty-foot Racer slides were the longest, tallest, fastest and scariest playground slides available. Every Burlington park playground had a slide, but only Ethan Allen Park had this behemoth.

The slide featured a steep (sixty-two degrees) double ladder up to a platform that stood fifteen feet off the ground. The Racer was a double slide, and it was called the Racer because two sliders could go down at the same time, racing to the bottom.

There was plenty of opportunity for kids to fall off the Racer. A child could fall off the ladder. The platform was enclosed by bars, but there was plenty of room between them for a child to fall through while horsing around waiting for their turn. And, of course, sliding down the steep, wavy slides

The two Racer slides that stood in the playground at Ethan Allen Park for decades provided memories for a lifetime for anyone who sped down them. *Courtesy of UVM Silver Special Collections.*

with very low guardrails presented the most likely scenario for a disoriented or scared slider to fall off.

And fall off they did. Every few years, an article appeared in the local papers about a child being injured falling off the Racer. Only the falls resulting in serious injuries made the papers, and they included falls resulting in a broken arm, a concussion and two broken wrists, among other injuries. But there were no mentions of lawsuits or payoffs, and the Racer slides did not come down. It was a different time. No city now would allow the installation of such a ride in one of its parks.

This memorable slide stood for decades but was finally taken down as it deteriorated and society became more litigious. For the many kids who sped down that slide over the years, the experience was unforgettable. People still talk about riding them to this day.

18

NEAR MISSES

I n researching the lost landmarks of Burlington for this book, I became keenly aware of how, for many years, historic preservation was not a factor in determining the fate of a building. The thought was that if you owned a building, you had the right to do whatever you wanted with it. Brief newspaper stories on the 1964 sale and destruction of the 1888 Howard Relief building were reported just like any other business transaction. Not a word was written about the irreplaceable architectural treasure that was about to be lost. When it became known that the Converse School was going to be torn down about the same time, there were a few reminiscences and regrets from former students. But the main attitude toward that case was that the building was inefficient and too far gone to save. Its removal was seen as "progress."

It was only after the destruction of New York City's Pennsylvania Station in the early 1960s that the historic preservation movement started to make ground in America. But it took many years before it became a force to be reckoned with across the country, including Burlington.

So it should come as no surprise that in addition to the losses covered in this book, Burlington came close to losing several other important buildings and properties. The demolition of each of the properties on this list was discussed seriously by city officials. Some came closer than others to the wrecking ball, but the fact that there was any suggestion at all from officials that any of these should be razed is stunning. Of course, we have the benefit of hindsight, but it's still hard to fathom how anyone in high office even back then could have thought for a minute that the removal of any of these buildings would have benefited Burlington.

EDMUNDS/BURLINGTON HIGH SCHOOL

Opened in 1900, the Italianate Edmunds High School building served as the city's high school until a new building opened in the mid-1960s off North Avenue. The 1900 building is rock solid over 120 years on and still serves as a school, the Edmunds Middle School.

Yet in 1962, Burlington superintendent of schools William T. Logan said that Edmunds should be taken down. He argued that the foundation was solid but that the rest of the structure, from the first floor to the roof, "was tired" and should be demolished. His plan was to use the basement for shop classes for the adjacent junior high school and build one story on top of the old foundation to house a cafeteria and more shop classrooms for the junior high.

This idea appears to have died a quick death, as no further mention of the plan to raze Edmunds has been found. Logan's desire to have the matter put to the voters never happened. The historic significance of Edmunds is recognized by its inclusion as part of the Main Street–College Street National Historic District. And the building is still not tired.

THE FLETCHER FREE LIBRARY

The 1904 Andrew Carnegie–funded Fletcher Free Library, which stands on the corner of College and South Winooski Avenue, was built on a portion of the Burlington ravine that was filled in over generations with trash, garbage, wood shavings and all other manner of debris. The use of improper fill caused the land under the building to settle, and by the early '70s, it had settled to the point that it was unsafe and could no longer be used. The books were removed to the basement of Memorial Auditorium. The library was in real danger of being demolished due to the high cost of shoring up the building. Even the library commission thought that demolition and a new library was the best way to go. But a group of local citizens led by Lillian Baker Carlisle and Marcella Chapman formed a group that mobilized to save the building. They got it added to the National

Register of Historic Places. A federal grant was obtained to stabilize the building, and in 1978, a $2.4 million bond issue was passed for repairs and an addition. The library was saved, and the books were returned for the grand reopening on January 4, 1981.

ETHAN ALLEN ENGINE COMPANY NO. 4 FIREHOUSE

The 1888 firehouse building was designed by prominent Burlington architect A.B. Fisher. It was constructed for the use of volunteer fire company Ethan Allen Engine Company No. 4, discussed in the section on the Ethan Allen Club.

But just a few years after the Ethans, as they were called, settled into their new firehouse, Burlington abandoned the old volunteer system and went with a paid fire department. For a number of years, the Ethans' fire station next door to City Hall on Church Street was rented to the fire department. When the department opened a new main fire station in 1929, the old firehouse became police headquarters.

In 1957, Burlington's city engineer condemned the building as unsafe, and the fire marshal said the building was a threat to employees and the public. A new police station was built, and as the time for the police to vacate the old firehouse approached, in 1965, the mayor made it clear that he was strongly in favor of demolition of the 1888 building.

In November 1966, the mayor stated that it would be torn down as soon as the police were moved out. He admitted that there was a proposal from an architect to save the building because of its architectural merit, but that while he agreed that it was an "interesting building," for economic and safety reasons he was opposed to any action other than its demolition. He said he wanted to see the building, which had been condemned as a structural and fire hazard, taken down and the site grassed over. In an editorial, the *Burlington Free Press* indicated that it agreed wholeheartedly with the mayor and that the sooner the firehouse was torn down, the better.

In fairness to the mayor, it does appear that he was the victim of some bad advice. In 1967, an architect examined the building and declared that it was structurally sound except for some needed repairs on the bell tower. This new information brought a six-month reprieve while other options were explored.

Finally, in 1969, the mayor announced that he had changed his mind and that demolishing the old firehouse was no longer an option. He said that he had heard from many people who loved the old station and did not want it torn down. The clincher, he said, was an extensive article about the firehouse written by Ada Louise Huxtable, the architecture editor of the *New York Times*. She stressed the aesthetic value that the firehouse brought to that end of Church Street.

So, after years on the endangered list, the firehouse was saved as common sense and good judgment prevailed. The tide was turning in favor of preservation. The building has had several tenants over the years and is now the Burlington City Arts Firehouse Gallery. The old firehouse is now in the National Register of Historic Places.

THE WINTERBOTHAM ESTATE

The so-called Winterbotham Estate, at the corner of South Willard and Main Streets, sprawls well down South Willard from the corner. It sits on a huge lot whose land slopes down sharply from the residence, still providing a panoramic view despite all of the building that has occurred in the two centuries since the estate was built. The original brick house dates to 1820, and the additions were made in the 1830s and '40s. A separate law office building was constructed in 1838.

The first portion was built by a man named James Potwin, and he sold the estate in the 1830s to Don Carlos Baxter, a prominent Burlington attorney. He built the law office, a mini–Greek Revival building. Later owners included the University of Vermont and John Winterbotham, a prominent art collector. The estate for a time was owned by the City of Burlington, which used it as the administrative headquarters of the School Department. It is now owned by Champlain College (Skiff Hall). It is commonly referred to as the Winterbotham Estate. The estate is important historically and architecturally.

Yet in the early 1960s, a committee was formed to study the possibility of demolishing the estate and erecting a new Chittenden County Courthouse on the site. The county judges presented this proposal to the Burlington School Board in March 1964. After this was reported in the local paper, numerous letters to the editor appeared expressing outrage at the idea that the city, not a private developer, would even think of destroying such an important Burlington landmark. Even the officials who were not opposed to demolishing the estate did not think that a bond issue required to carry out the proposal had any chance of passing.

So the proposal died a fairly quick death. In 1972, the city drew up a list of sixty-three important buildings in the city worthy of preservation. The Winterbotham Estate was one of the properties listed. It is now listed in the National Register of Historic Places.

CONCLUSION

Things change, time passes and the new replaces the old. It's the story of America. Steamboats, canal boats, passenger trains and trolley cars all had their day and were vital parts of the fabric of Burlington for many years. The industrial waterfront came and went. You can't preserve everything, and you wouldn't want to.

For many years, this was the way people viewed classic, old buildings. The old makes way for the new, and the modern and efficient replaces the outdated and inefficient. As numerous examples have shown, no matter how historic or beautiful a building was, those things often were not enough to save them from demolition in the name of progress. The Converse School, the Louisa Howard Mission House, the old Lawrence Barnes School—all fell to the wrecking ball with barely a peep of protest.

The destruction of McKim, Mead & White's monumental Pennsylvania Station in Manhattan is widely viewed as the beginning of the historic preservation movement. That act of civic vandalism appalled and shocked many, and not just in New York City. People all across America began to wake up to the fact that the buildings being taken down were irreplaceable, that what was being put up in their place was often a very poor substitute. There won't be another Gothic cathedral built in Burlington, or a school like Converse, or a Strong Theatre. It took many years for this point of view to spread to the majority of citizens in Burlington: that there are certain unique structures that must be protected because they are historic, beautiful and irreplaceable.

It's complicated. There are property rights to consider. The rights of a property owner cannot be ignored. And preserving large, old, ornate buildings is expensive, beyond the ability of all but a few individuals and institutions. Striking a balance is difficult, but the pendulum has swung firmly to the side of historic preservation. That 1972 list of sixty-three city buildings worthy of preservation was the first concrete step taken by the city on the road to preserving remaining city landmarks. Certainly, today there is a long list of Burlington buildings that no one would even dare to mention as possible candidates for demolition.

Other steps have been taken over the years. Hundreds of Burlington buildings are listed in the National Register of Historic Places or as part of National Historic Districts. The city has its own list of historic buildings, structures designated as historic beyond those that have been placed in national registers. The so-called Five Sisters neighborhood is an example of this. Things have changed for the better as regards protecting historic buildings in Burlington, although some argue that the pendulum has swung too far in favor of preservation.

As stated previously, Burlington is lucky to have many of its historic properties in the hands of the University of Vermont and Champlain College, both of which have done an admirable job of preservation combined with tasteful adaptation for the large inventory of great old buildings under their stewardship.

The city is also lucky to have the Shelburne Museum located just a few miles down the road. Founder Electra Havemeyer Webb had the vision, the commitment and, most important, the resources to carry out some prodigious work of historic preservation. As a result of her efforts, the 1906 side-wheeler steamboat *Ticonderoga*, an important part of the history of Burlington (and America), sits in good hands on the museum grounds. The *Ti* is the last walking beam steamboat remaining of the thousands that used to ply the waterways of America. Joining it in Shelburne are the Colchester Reef Lighthouse, the old Rutland Railroad Shelburne depot, along with a Rutland locomotive and cars sitting beside the depot. Undoubtedly all would have been scrapped but for Mrs. Webb.

And, as stated previously, Burlington's inventory of historic homes is remarkably intact (the urban renewal zone excepted, of course). Many may have been subdivided into apartments, but the streetscapes of many of Burlington's old streets have not changed all that much since the homes were built.

Where Burlington has not been lucky is with fires. The plague of fire has visited the city often. Of the buildings discussed in this book, twenty were lost to flames. There was a huge spate of fires in the city in the 1970s. One or more arsonists set some of those blazes. No one will ever know how many. But the toll is huge: four downtown hotels, the two cathedrals, two of the three yacht clubs and on and on. Modern fire prevention measures, chiefly sprinkler systems, have done much to eliminate large fires in Burlington. The last major fire in downtown Burlington was the 1974 Centers fire. A side benefit of sprinkler systems is that they have enabled the removal of the many fire escapes that used to be found on large buildings, such as the Richardson and the Masonic Temple. Their removal certainly enhances the look of many old structures.

To sum up, much has been lost in Burlington, but much remains needing protection. There are no guarantees, of course, but the steps needed to protect the city from future losses have been taken. Historic designations and required approval by city boards and commissions ensure that historic buildings cannot be removed without thorough review and oversight. The threat posed by fire has been largely eliminated by technology. And probably most important, public awareness and appreciation for the importance of historic structures to the community has come full circle. From what used to be near universal public apathy, or the idea that progress and property rights trump everything else, this new awareness is probably the best protection that Burlington's architectural heritage could have. There is now a long list of structures in the city that no one would dream of proposing for demolition. The public wouldn't have it.

BIBLIOGRAPHY

Allen, Charles E. *About Burlington Vermont*. Burlington, VT: Hobart J. Shanley & Co., 1905.

Annual Reports of the City of Burlington Vermont.

Auld, Joseph. *Picturesque Burlington*. Burlington: Burlington Vermont Free Press Association, 1894.

Burlington Daily News archives. newspapers.com.

Burlington Free Press archives. newspapers.com.

Champlain Transportation Company. *The Steamboats of Lake Champlain, 1809–1930*. Albany, NY: Champlain Transportation Company, 1930.

Cohn, Arthur B. *Lake Champlain's Sailing Canal Boats*. Vergennes, VT: Lake Champlain Maritime Museum, 2003.

Crockett, Walter Hill. *A History of Lake Champlain*. Burlington, VT: Hobart J. Shanley & Co., 1909.

Daniels, Robert V. *The University of Vermont: The First 200 Years*. Lebanon, NH: University Press of New England, 1991.

Defebaugh, James Elliott. *History of the Lumber Industry of America*. Chicago: The American Lumberman, 1906.

Frank Leslie's Illustrated Newspaper.

Hawthorne, Nathaniel. *Hawthorne's American Travel Sketches*. Lebanon, NH: University Press of New England, 1989.

Herndon, Richard, ed. *Men of Progress*. Boston, MA: New England Press, 1889.

Hill, Ralph Nading. "Lake Champlain: Key to Liberty." *Vermont Life Magazine*, 1977.

James, Henry. *Travels with Henry James*. New York: Nation Books, 2016.

Keenan, Robert G., and Reverend Francis R. Prive. *The History of St. Joseph Parish from 1830 to 1987*. Burlington, VT: St. Joseph Church, 1988.

Library of Congress. Detroit Publishing Company photograph collection.

Possons, Charles H. *Vermont, Its Resources and Industries*. N.p.: C.H. Possons Publisher, 1889.

Schmeckebier, Laurence. *The Customs Service, Its History, Activities and Organization*. Baltimore, MD: Johns Hopkins University Press, 1924.

Stone, Arthur Fairbanks. *The Vermont of Today*. New York: Lewis Historical Publishing Company, 1929.

ABOUT THE AUTHOR

B
ob Blanchard was born and raised in the South End of Burlington, Vermont. He was educated in Burlington's Catholic school system and graduated from the University of Vermont with a degree in history. After a thirty-five-year career with the U.S. Customs Service in Vermont and New York, he took up local history as a serious hobby. His Burlington Area History Facebook group has found a large audience for its daily postings. After publishing several articles, *Lost Burlington, Vermont* is his first book. He currently resides in St. Albans, Vermont.

Visit us at
www.historypress.com